becoming a designer

Ruth Artmonsky

Published by:
Artmonsky Arts
Flat 1, 27 Henrietta Street
London WC2E 8NA
artmonskyruth@gmail.com
Tel. 07767 820 406

Text © Ruth Artmonsky 2022

ISBN 978-1-9163845-6-9

Designed by:
David Preston Studio
www.davidprestonstudio.com

Printed in Wales by:
Gomer Press
https://gomerprinting.co.uk

My thanks to Eduardo
Sant'Anna for his help with the
images and to David Preston
Studio for their enthusiasm and
imaginative book design.

contents

foreword

In my twenties I got a job as a research assistant in an institute whilst studying to become a psychologist. I was either at my desk before a large calculator (operated by turning a handle), or researching in the well-stocked library. It was in the library one day that I came upon a bulky book, and, although now I can neither remember the title nor the author, I can still remember the format of its' contents. It set out to describe the childhood and youth of geniuses, of people in history who had been distinguished by their achievements, and thereby try to understand, or at least find common ground, in their precocity. Can one discern genius in advance?

Since then my interests have drifted from psychology to design, but I have, from time to time, considered compiling something similar for the many exceptional personalities I have come across in this broad field – from textiles and fashion, through graphics and typography, to three dimensional design. Can one predict exceptional design talent?

Now I realise that, although still eager to tackle such research, I have neither the time left nor the stamina, but undaunted, I decided to attempt at least a 'taster', in the hopes that some future researcher in the area of design history may take up and run with the idea.

I have not adopted an arbitrary age as to when a young person could have begun to call themselves 'designer', but have tended to run down my accounts of their lives when I feel they have their feet not timorously but firmly on the design ladder, for that time differs widely between individuals.

In bringing together the early lives of designers in diverse fields I have borrowed blatantly from the works of diligent biographers who have oftime spent years searching through diaries and correspondence and interviewing countless relatives, friends and cognoscenti. I have, I hope, acknowledged all these worthies in the extensive bibliography.

design as a profession

What I am saying is that in solving many of the real and exciting problems posed by the twentieth century, the designer – just as much as the scientist, the engineer, the doctor or the teacher – has an important part to play.

Designers should not sit in the wings waiting to be asked to take the stage … as members of society, designers, I suggest, should actively campaign for recognition of the role they ought to play.

Herbert Spencer, *The Penrose Annual*, 1964

Opposite: Harry Thubron conducting a class in basic design at Leeds School of Art, c. 1961.

The term 'design' was actually used by the British Government as early as the 1830s, when it established the Government School of Design, which was to morph eventually into the Royal College of Art; but 'design', as a profession, was very much a twentieth century phenomenon.

The Government would tend to show concern for the design of goods whenever there was a down turn in the economy, when overseas competition was threatening, when all was not right, with lulls of interest in between. At times of impending crisis there would be a flurry of activity, and the Board of Trade, or whatever the relevant department was termed at that time, would set up commissions of inquiry, and such like, to pinpoint where the trouble lay and what could be done about it.

Much of this activity, incidentally, raised awareness of design, particular when it was decided to show off what the country could produce of a competitive standard. From the 'Great Exhibition' of 1851 to the post-WWII exhibitions as 'Britain Can Make It' in 1946, and beyond, the proliferation of exhibitions, both national and international, clearly provided opportunities for creative young minds to test themselves. But beyond stirring an awareness of design in manufacturers and the population in general, these show off spectacles did little actually to gain recognition of design as a valid career. Even when the Government's Council of Industrial Design was established in 1944, its function was largely educating taste rather than directly validating the profession of designer.

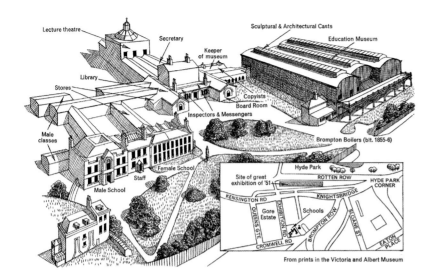

Above: Government School of Design (original site of the Royal College of Art).

Above right: Monthly journal of the Society of Industrial Artists, June 1939.

When a group of interested people – manufacturers, retailers, artists and designers – gathered together in 1915 to form the Design & Industries Association (DIA), actually adopting the word 'design' in its title, some time before it ever appeared in the syllabus of any educational institution, the organisation recognised the need for the formal training of designers. In an early memorandum DIA gave a nod to training needs but was not, as an organisation, to become evangelical about it:

In England…commerce and art education remain two separate and unyielding and opposing activities. This condition makes for a sterility of education and the degradation of commerce. It is desirable, above all things to bring the two

Opposite left: Guide for the
Council of Industrial Design
travelling exhibition, designed
by James Gardner.

Opposite right: Council
of Industrial Design logo,
designed by Hans Schleger.
As featured on the front
cover of *Design* magazine,
October 1955.

into true relationship so that education may become
a preparation for commerce, and commerce the fulfillment
of education.

In spite of this concern, the DIA, with the aim 'to encourage a
more intelligent demand amongst the public for what is best and
soundest', mainly translated this into proselytizing by publications,
exhibitions, lectures, conferences, and such. By the mid-1930s it
began to run out of steam, on which McKnight Kauffer, the major
graphic designer in England at the time, put down to it being: 'very
gentlemanly in its habits, it has had too much good taste'.

It was not until the 1930s that those who were actually themselves designing, felt sufficiently confident to band together to define
and defend what they did, and, even then, they did not choose to
use the word 'design' when considering a name – the Society of
Industrial Artists (SIA). Nevertheless this was the earliest attempt
in Britain, to give design a professional status. The organisation's
Articles of Association stated:

> The Society should establish itself as a professional associa-
> tion which would aim at being a controlling authority to
> advance and protect the interests of Industrial Artists and at
> raising the standard of Industrial Art in this country, both
> from an economic and industrial standpoint. An organisa-
> tion that would be responsible for establishing standards of

practice and conduct, and one that would act as a liaison between Artists and the Industrialist.

James Holland, in his history of the Society, wrote that at the time of its inception it was a very bold concept to think that there could be:

> ...a critical common factor linking the publicity designer, the interior designer, the fashion designer and the engineering product designer.

Although SIA never achieved the firm control on its professionals as, say, the Royal Institute of British Architecture, it was energetically active on behalf of its members – liaising with relevant organisations, setting up regional offshoots, producing its own publication to keep its 'professionals' au fait with matters relating to design, and setting its own standards for accepting members.

Soon SIA was adopting all the pompous accoutrements of a well-established professional body – annual conferences, design orations, medals of merit, and the like. Yet it was not until the 1960s that the word 'design' was considered key to its image when, in 1963 it became the Society of Industrial Artists and Designers, and its journal was renamed *The Designer*.

When it came to the matter of developing young designers, although SIA had its own standards for accepting them as student members, it would tend to make an organisational response when

NOTHING NEED BE UGLY

Raymond Plummer

Foreword by Sir Monty Finniston FRS

consulted on matters of education and training rather than being evangelically proactive.

Although all this activity generally raised awareness of design as key to the welfare of the country and its economy it was largely left to whatever government department that had responsibility for education, variously named over the years, to find ways of effectively training young would-be designers who sought to develop their skills through formal education.

The initial aim of the early Government School of Design, implicit in its title, got diluted over the years as the School veered towards 'fine' art and art teacher training. Its name changed, in 1853, to the National Art Training School, and then, eventually to the Royal College of Art, 'design' totally erased.

The Education Act of 1902 gave the newly established Local Educational Authorities responsibility for their art schools, and some, particularly those where there was a specific local industry, did offer related courses. Yet by the 1930s the Gorrell Report rather diplomatically understated the situation: 'It is common knowledge, we believe, that co-operation between Industry and Art Schools is not always so close as it should be.'

Henry Cole, who in the mid-nineteenth century, for some twenty years, was responsible for twenty three Schools of Design nationally, had striven to create an ethos of co-operation between school and manufacturer. In London, William Lethaby, into the twentieth century, initially as Art Inspector to the Technical

Education Board, and then working at Central School of Arts & Crafts and at the Royal College, did what he could to spread the gospel that art education should embrace industrialisation.

However, what individual efforts, thereafter, had been made in a similar direction at individual colleges, the position of design as a course or subject in its own right, did not really become standard practice until after WWII when, in 1946, the Ministry of Education introduced the National Diploma in Design (NDD), and then, after what came to be known as the Coldstream Report, in 1961, the Diploma in Art & Design (Dip. AD). What had been the position before this can be appreciated by the fact that when colleges sought approval for running Dip. AD courses, at the first tranch of applications, only sixty-one out of two-hundred and one art and design courses were accepted as reaching the required standard.

Even with national standards set there were inevitably marked differences between colleges, and between design course within any college, as to the balance given to theoretical versus 'hands-on', to general broad education versus specialisation, to meeting market needs versus experiment, and to practical compromise versus ego trips.

What does this add up to when considering the development of the young designers included here. Some had to, or chose to, make their own way with little, if any, formal education; others enrolled on courses but found them wanting; yet others found well-designed courses and/or, inspiring teachers. One way or another they became professional designers, with their design excellence recognised by honorary degrees, ranges of letters after their names, medals and such. By the 1950s design had become a profession that was recognised and rewarded.

becoming a textile or fashion designer

In art colleges, early courses in textile and fashion design tended to be grouped together in one department. Yet although textile and fashion designers clearly need a knowledge and understanding of each others' work, it is rare for any designer to have his or her foot in both camps. And even when it comes to developing a career in textiles alone there are those students more interested in fibres and the weaving of the cloth and those more interested in patterning its surface; the weaving end obviously lies closer to the manufacturing process, the patterning to 'art'.

The British textile industry was slow to appreciate the crucial role design could contribute to profitability. It was only when it was becoming trounced by overseas competitors with cheaper production costs, that the industry began to see design as a commercial weapon. As a result, apart from the odd employee trying to make his or her way towards a more creative job as well as they could within the industry, or the odd free-lance, largely

Opposite: Fashion design students from the Royal College of Art, 1967.

21

Left: Mary Oliver and John Drummond, textile printing, Central School of Arts and Crafts, 1949.

self-educated designer, trying to infiltrate from outside, the training and development of textile designers was largely left to educational establishments – technical colleges and art schools. Even then, many manufacturers were reluctant to offer employees day-release and many employees, if they wanted to develop their talents, were obliged to attend evening classes at their own expense.

Although technical colleges (to morph into polytechnics and then universities), particularly those in textile manufacturing areas as Glasgow, Galashiels, Manchester, Leeds, Huddersfield and Leicester, offered textile related courses, few included design as subject matter (let alone as a subject in its own right) until after World War II.

One of a handful of exceptions was Leeds University, which, by the 1930s had built up an international reputation for its textile technology courses. Tibor Reich, a major textile designer in Britain in the post-war years, from his basic training in his homeland of Hungary, studied at Leeds in the late '30s, where he received awards for his handloom woven patterns.

In London art schools the would-be woven cloth designer, in the pre-war and immediate post-war years, benefited from a remarkable clutch of tutors, such as Ronald Grierson at Camberwell College of Art, and Dora Batty, first at Camberwell and then at Central School of Arts and Crafts, with Marianne Straub in charge of weaving classes. Straub offered a sensitively graded course:

> Let them do plain weave. Let them get the beauty of plain cloths first and use each yarn separately and then use them in conjunction.

Taking a broad view of the training of textile designers, Alec Hunter, when a Director of Warner & Son considered that it was the responsibility of the art college that:

> ...the textile student should be taught to draw; to construct cloth; to sense the qualities of fibres and to know their qualities; to develop an ability to use 'colour'.

The art colleges tended to blame the textile manufacturers for their conservatism when it came to employing or commissioning designers but the formidable Margaret Leischner, at the Royal College of Art into the 1960s, lay some of the blame on the colleges themselves:

> The attitude of Art Schools has been largely instrumental in hindering the development of woven design in this country. It is regarded as a 'craft', or, like embroidery, as a women's craft which provides opportunity for self-expression. It does, in fact, require a very high degree of professionalism…in woven fabrics the total appeal comes from an inherent understanding of decorative qualities combined with a fundamental understanding of production methods and end uses.

When Alastair Morton of Morton Sundour was commissioned by the Colour, Design and Style Centre of the Cotton Board, in Manchester, to carry out a survey of the teaching of textile design in art institutions he added another unhelpful attitude of the colleges, as he found that their Principals invariably, and actively, dissuaded their students from seeking positions in the textile industry because of its abysmally low rates of pay and positions offered.

With the expense and room space necessary for the training of designers of woven textiles, many art colleges were inclined to focus

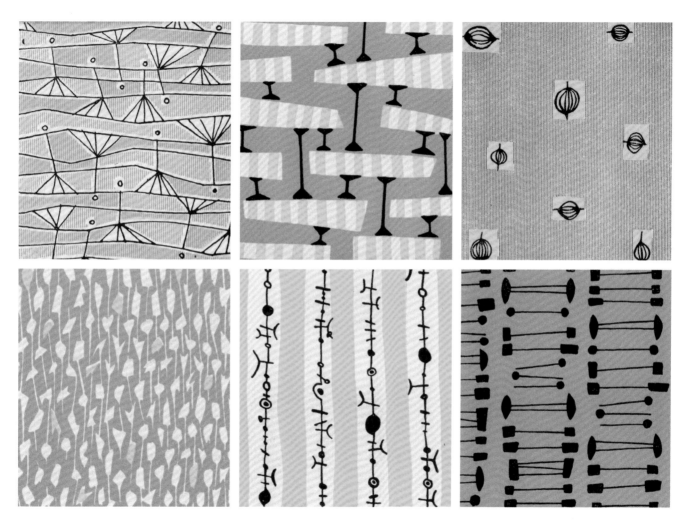

A selection of student textile designs, Royal College of Art, 1960s.

more on printed surface design. It is recorded that Glasgow School of Art was offering such courses from its inception in the nineteenth century. Often printed textile courses were little more than fine art courses, with printing done on material rather than paper (initially by hand-blocking, and then by silk screening), they were closely allied to 'fine' art departments.

How close this was is exemplified by Lucienne Day, the major British surface designer of the post-war years, being utterly bored by what was going on in the Fine Art Department at the Royal College of Art and what was expected of her, when she studied there at the end of the 1930s, compared to the stimulation found by the likes of Barbara Brown, Althea McNish and Doreen Dyall. Under the tutorship of Humphrey Spender – 'a joy' – students were learning repeats, colour separations, and transferring and printing techniques in the increasingly experimental and 'Pop' art period there in the post-war years.

Even with surface design there was some friction between colleges and manufacturers. A representative of Horrockses, a major textile and fashion company was to complain:

I think that the College student should not only produce designs which are preconceived by himself but should also be taught to create textile designs in which the problem is set by the public, the trend of fashion, or by the wishes of the potential customer or employer. I don't think being forced to

26

work on a particular theme, not chosen by himself, would lower the artistic standards of the student's work. It would give him self-discipline, and he would still find himself able to express himself within limitations.

As with most design training, the dilemma was, and perhaps still is, how to balance the needs of the manufacturer in relation to capital investment and market fluctuations, and the needs of the would-be design student to express him- or her-self, explore, experiment and pioneer.

If textile design was considered little more than a woman's hobby rather than a profession, fashion design fared worse, being considered, in addition, ephemeral, shallow, and superficial. There was barely any formal training for fashion designers as such until the late 1940s. 'Needle trades' were originally catered for by junior and senior 'trade' schools; in London those in the East End, with students largely drawn from immigrant families, feeding the 'rag' trade, those in the West End feeding 'haute couture'.

A 1924 Board of Education Report on the Barrett Street trade school, near Selfridges (that was to become the London College of Fashion), summarised the aim of the school:

> …to enable girls to enter certain of the London trades which necessitated a high standard of skill, intelligence, initiative, originality, and artistic perception in order that the standard

27

of production required by the public may be maintained and a successful career for the individual assured.

This appears to hint at some upward route available to junior dress-makers, possibly towards a design role given the attributes listed. Yet when, in the late 1930s, Muriel Pemberton considered changing her fine art studies at the Royal College of Art to dress design-ing she was obliged to build up a course for herself as the College lacked one. The College did have some kind of 'dress' department, run for some twenty years by a Mrs Gibson, but with the arrival of Robin Darwin in 1948 she was soon shown the door.

It was only in the post-war years that the professional training of fashion designers really developed with Pemberton's makeshift course for herself morphing into a pioneer course at St. Martin's, and with Madge Garland's and Janey Ironside's more high profile courses at the Royal College. Yet still a stigma surrounded this design speciality as the College 'fashion' depart-ment was isolated from the new building, and, for some time, it was denied the degree status offered in the other College's design departments – fashion did not fit Darwin's snobbish aspirations for his institution.

The dressmaking classes that had existed at the Central School of Arts and Crafts from the time it moved into its Holborn building, became a school of costume in its own right in 1930. Steered by Jeanette Cochran, this veered towards the theatrical,

Right: Dressmaking students from Barrett Street trade school, 1930s.

eventually becoming a broad theatre design course diverging from the fashion world.

Until the 1950s fashion designers had largely to make their own way, either working with couturiers or within manufacturing companies, or, if with enough hutzpah and sufficient finance, setting up on their own, as did Laura Ashley (who had only had a secretarial training), and Mary Quant (who had studied illustration at Goldsmith's College).

enid marx

1902—1998

When asked how her interest in textiles originated Enid Marx spoke vaguely of there having been trading in cloth with her mother's forebears, and of her grandmother teaching her to look critically at materials – neither suggestion sufficiently substantial to account for what was to become her life's work. In fact Marx's interests in textiles did not emerge at all clearly until the end of her student days and would come from a variety of sources in combination.

Marx came from a comfortably off middle class family, her mother born in England to German emigres, her father born in Germany. Her father's business was in paper technology, but his inventiveness went way beyond this, with a wide variety of patents to his name. He would occasionally take Marx on visits to factories, albeit it would prove to be a good number of years before she would find herself dealing directly with the textile industry as such.

A more direct influence on young Marx was her sister Daisy, older by some twelve years. Daisy was a woman of some spirit – private secretary to the Vice-principal of L'Institute Francaise, contributing to it's development, and a line manager in the wartime Ministry of Food. Her various activities merited an obituary in *The Times*, and, for Marx, she provided a role model of an independent woman making a career for herself. It was Daisy, with her French connections, who brought back for Marx French folk art prints from wood blocks that showed her for the first time what wood block printing could produce.

Right: Enid Marx wood engraving from the Royal College of Art magazine *Gallimaufry*, 1925.

WOODCUT.   MARX.

Left: Shield designs by Marx for London Underground seating, showing the original drawn artwork and the woven textile, 1930s–40s.

Marx started her education at South Hampstead High School but did not fit in and it was decided she should board at Roedean, where it was thought the sea air would be of benefit to her. Roedean, at the time, was not a school that aimed high academically but one offering a reasonably liberal education. Marx, who had found problems with the written word at her previous school, soon found her niche there in the art room and carpentry shop. She later wrote:

> I did life drawing, cut stencils, printed stuffs, made pots, as well as doing miscellaneous drawings. I may say I was not particularly efficient at drawing, only passionately interested.

And there we have the nub of Marx's development as a designer, for it was at Roedean she set her mind on becoming an artist, in spite of lacking the necessary talent. Nevertheless, on leaving Roedean in 1921, Marx, with her parent's support, applied to the Royal College of Art, and specifically to the Painting School. Not surprisingly her portfolio failed to reach the required standard.

Determined to reapply she decided to spend the intervening year at the Central School of Arts and Crafts, in Holborn, with Bernard Meninsky teaching her drawing, Edward Johnstone calligraphy and Lindsay Butterfield textiles. Marx was scathing about the teaching, felt alien to her fellow students, and found some solace in visiting the nearby Poetry Bookshop, which familiarised her with hand-blocked chapbooks, and the Museum of Mankind which started her interest in primitive artefacts, particularly early printing on bark cloth.

At a second attempt Marx was accepted at the Royal College, where, beyond her actual course, she found compatible friends and mentors, some of whom were to prove useful in her career development. Paul Nash encouraged her to wood-engrave when Frank Short banned her from his classes as 'unable to draw' and 'not worth teaching'. On receiving this news Marx took herself off to Leon Underwood's school for wood-engraving so determined was she to develop her skills in this medium.

Unsurprisingly Marx failed her examination in painting, she would later claim because of the vulgarity of the subject she chose. It was in fact her patterning from engraving, rather than her

drawing, that got her her first commission from the Curwen Press for end papers (whilst she was still at college). It was only when a friend, Norah Braden, took her to see an exhibition of hand-blocked textiles produced by Phyllis Baron and Dorothy Larcher that, in a flash, as it were, she saw how her interest in wood-engraving could be used for textile design. She immediately arranged a visit to Baron and Larcher in Hampstead and persuaded them to take her on as an apprentice.

> I wasn't allowed to write down any recipes
> – I used to memorise them and rush home
> and write them down later. In their work-
> shop I used to hose velvet to get the chalk
> out, stir the gum, rinse and stir again.

Marx later complained about the drudgery of the tasks she was given with Baron and Larcher, however, she absorbed sufficient knowledge and practical know-how to have the confidence to set up on her own. By the late 1920s and into the 1930s Marx began to make a name for herself for her geometric hand-blocked textile designs, selling at boutique shops run by friends, as that of Cecilia

Dunbar, who she had known at the Royal College, or showing at exhibitions at home and abroad, again frequently riding on the backs of friends as Paul Nash, Michael Cardew and Katherine Pleydell-Bouverie.

Alan Powers, her biographer, wrote that by 1930, at the age of 28, Marx had definitely 'arrived'. Yet it could be argued that much of her 'getting herself about' to what Marx described as 'an exclusive market' was via friends. She really, independently, got her foot on her career ladder when she was commissioned to provide designs for manufactured textiles for London Transport in the late 1930s, and had to cope with 'real' life, with textiles for travelling Londoners and all that implied, and with manufacturers daring to modify her designs to fit their production operations. Overcoming such challenges brought Marx an altogether wider recognition as did her role with textiles in the Government's wartime Utility Scheme. It was as a 'Pattern Maker' that she was recognised when becoming a Royal Designer for Industry in 1944.

alastair morton

1910—1963

Alastair Morton grew up immersed in the textile industry. His grandfather and his father were not only entrepreneurs running a successful textile company – Morton Sundour – but were both experimental, innovative men, interested in textile manufacturing as a technical challenge as well as a business.

Morton's brother, Jocelyn, writing a history of the company, described Alastair as a boy as being interested in everything, musical, academic, an all-rounder, who became Head Boy of his enlightened co-educational school (St. George's School, Harpenden). There had been no specific plan for Morton to join the family firm, albeit his father had given him for his fifteenth birthday a book, 'Weaving and other pleasant occupations'

and had inscribed it 'to A.M. The Prentice Weaver, Nov. 1925'.

In fact Morton started a mathematics degree at Edinburgh University, leaving after a year to study at Balliol College, Oxford. Whether he was unsure of the direction he was taking, or whether he thought he need an income as he was planning to get married, after a year at Balliol he suddenly left, announcing to his father, James, that he wanted to join the company, and to his mother: 'I'm getting more and more restless to start doing something on the face of the earth and not only in the air.'

Given Morton's mathematical ability and interests it was thought he would be would want to be involved in the scientific research that was going on in the firm, but he wanted 'to dabble at

Alastair Morton, 1937.

everything'. He not only set out to study the whole technical process of textile manufacture but also applied himself to understanding the commercial aspects of the industry as well. He wrote of himself at that time:

> I had not intended to be a designer, yet as I was most interested in that side of manufacturing I became more and more absorbed by it ... another horrid example to shock the educational authorities of a designer drifting into his job without previous selection, training or qualifications.

Morton joined the family firm in 1932. He had, indeed, not shown any previous interest in, or talent for drawing and painting; it would seem that in his early twenties it just emerged 'ready made'! The company had its own studio headed by Frank Gibson, and in the year he joined, young Morton was fortunate enough to be allowed to accompany his father and Gibson on what could be termed a designer's 'grand tour' – a trip to the Continent visiting designers and craft ateliers. Incidentally it was on this trip that he first met Hans Aufseer (later anglicised to Tisdall), who he would later be commissioning.

Soon Morton was seeking out artists to commission. Jocelyn Morton wrote of him:

> Alastair found that he had inherited, in certainly undiluted, possibly even intensified, from his grandfather and father, that gift of creative insight that enabled all three of them to conceive new textile forms.

With growing confidence, both of the art world and of the weaving process, Morton began not only to commission designers , but to apply himself to translate commissioned works into production-ready designs. Even when challenged with one of Ben Nicholson's monotone-bas-relief, by a clever combination of weave and different qualities of yarn, all of them white, he got it ready for production.

In 1928, the firm had set up a subsidiary, Edinburgh Weavers, targeting interior designers and architects. Its mission statement read:

> ... we should aim at fabrics that not have only a temporary fashion, but from their construction of weave, beauty of design or colouring, might be considered of continuing interest for persons of knowledge and taste.

It was to be the up-market arm of the family firm and the area in which Morton's talents were to develop, initially in interpreting others' designs, but then beginning to design himself. Jocelyn considered the 'interpretation' as much a creative process as producing an original design.

> Alastair, when faced with an artist's work which he wished to translate into a textile, would contemplate it for weeks, sometimes for months, before he was satisfied with the right weaves, the right yarns, the best printing technique, the necessary blend of coloured yarns, to give a true interpretation.

Now at the helm of Edinburgh Weavers, Morton began to attract prestigious commissions and to show at international exhibitions. Although he found himself increasing involved in general

Right: Alastair Morton textile design for Edinburgh Weavers.

Printed Hanging

AFM
Nov 12th 39

Hand looms at Ethel Mairet's workshop, Ditchling, c. 1935.

management by now he was set on being Design Director, or, as he termed the role, Styling Director. He even took time out to study hand spinning and weaving with Ethel Mairet, the distinguished craft weaver in Ditchling, after which he set up a loom for himself at home, designing both for the company and for other textile firms, as Horrockses. He was also drawn into educating people on design in his industry, lecturing and carrying out a survey on textile design education for the Cotton Board.

Before he was thirty Morton had, through his own motivation and efforts, developed into a textile designer. With his own designs he decided initially to be anonymous, but, with increasing confidence, he began to let his name be attached. One might see the years up to the onset of war as his 'apprenticeship'.

Morton's talents, both as interpreter and original designer, were rewarded by his becoming a Fellow of the Society of Industrial Designers in 1947, and a Royal Designer of Industry in 1960. His death from heart problems at the age of fifty-three was untimely. Gordon Russell in his obituary of Morton wrote:

His true humility, friendliness, and generosity, made it possible for him to recognise, employ and encourage other designers, all of whom liked working for one whose ability in their sphere they acknowledged and whose integrity was never in doubt.

terence conran

1931–2020

Although, nowadays, best remembered as a furniture designer, retailer and restaurateur, Terence Conran started his career as a textile designer. Conran was born in Esher and brought up in London. His father was a merchant of fluctuating fortunes, his mother a frustrated housewife who had been sent to secretarial college when she had wanted to go to art school. The family, described as living in 'genteel semi-poverty', nevertheless seemed to be able to afford him receiving a private school education.

From his early years Conran was a doer, a self-starter with passionate interests – a collector of plants, butterflies and moths, and, more relevant for his inclusion here, a maker of things. As his biographer Nicholas Ind wrote: 'It was through the physical reality of making things, of working as a craftsman, that he came to design.'

Conran, a self-contained child, set up his own workshop at home, initially making models (some of which he sold to fellow pupils); eventually it came to be furnished with a kiln, a wheel, a lathe and facilities for screen printing.

Conran did not fare well in the various preparatory schools he attended and seemed to lack the intellectual calibre to go on to the public schools they fed into. His parents decision to send him to Bryanston for his secondary school education, could not have been bettered, for its focus on artistic and manual skills along with a conventional academic syllabus suited Conran exactly. He had stimulating teachers encouraging his interests in

Right: The young Terence Conran, featured alongside Jacqueline Groag in a press advertisement for David Whitehead Fabrics, 1953.

A Marian Mahler design on spun rayon, 48" wide. Available in bright red, blue-green, tan, grey, and green.

Designed by Terence Conran, available in four colour combinations on a white background. Spun rayon, 48" wide.

A design by Terence Conran, on spun rayon, 48" wide. Available with grey, beige or pale green predominating.

A design by Jacqueline Groag on backgrounds of bright red, blue-green, tan, grey, and green. Spun rayon, 48" wide.

These furnishing fabrics have *all* the virtues. Their colours are fresh and clear, their designs new and individual; they're guaranteed fast to sunlight and washing (Lux Washability Certificate). All this, yet their prices are in most cases under 10/- a yard, 48 inches wide.

DAVID WHITEHEAD FABRICS

Whether you want to bring new gaiety into an old room, or are furnishing for the first time, ask to see David Whitehead furnishing fabrics. Besides those shown here, they make a complete range in every style and type, at prices from 5/11d.

45

pottery, metal work and such; he made illustrations for the school magazine; and he won an engineering prize. He prospered in the areas that interested him and the fact that he was asked to leave came down to a technicality of his not having a light for his bike – a police matter.

Leaving school, Conran had no clear idea of what he wanted to do and it was his art master who, struck by Conran's skill with patterning and colour, and the fact that he had actually passed general science in his school certificate, suggested textile design. Conran had little of direct relevance to show the severe Head of Textiles at the Central School of Arts and Crafts to which he applied:

> I think Miss Batty was more interested in the scope of what I had done, rather than the quality of the work, although it was reasonably good – certainly the pottery was.

In 1948, the sixteen year old Conran started his three year textile design course at Central, which, focused as it was on learning by doing, suited him, much as Bryanston had done. Commuting from home, now in Liphook, Conran, not a natural socialiser, took what he would from his course, experimenting at home alone in his workshop.

It was the arrival of Eduardo Paolozzi at the end of Conran's first term that was to change things. Although Paolozzi was only temporarily attached to the textile department as tutor, the two immediately bonded and, indeed, were to remain friends long after Conran had left the College, the tutor taking the role of a substitute father. Paolozzi was newly arrived from Paris and was to extend Conran's horizons beyond suburbia to both the European and African art worlds, the former contemporary, the latter native. Conran now 'bubbling with ideas', began to design textiles inspired by his tutor's enthusiasm for African native art, but also by the work of such Europeans as Paul Klee, Juan Miro and Wassily Kandinsky.

At Central, Conran can be said to have developed self-discipline, so essential for design work, under the eagle eye of Dora Batty; to have acquired his know-how of textiles from Robert Addington (who coming from a textile family had only just completed his own training at Central); and to have been stimulated intellectually by Anton Ehrenzweig, who was to distinguish himself by

Conran, when he was a young textile designer.

linking psychoanalysis to art and design. Conran, not much more than seventeen, began to print and sell his own designs whilst still at College, much as he had sold his models whilst at school. He also got 'real' life experience assisting tutors with their commissions, as working with Ehrenzweig for the Aschers with their unique scarf designs, and with a colossal mural.

By his third year, when he had to choose between woven and printed fabric design he opted for the latter. Conran recorded:

> My whole attitude to design was really formed in those couple of years – about why shouldn't design be something that is available to the entire community.

It was in Conran's third year that Dennis Lennon, the architect and designer, visited Central and was struck by the originality and quality of Conran's work. He immediately offered him a job, and Conran, feeling he could learn more in a work situation that at college, accepted.

Lennon was not only running a private practice but was Director of the Rayon Design Centre.

Conran's 'Mobiles' design for Edinburgh Weavers, 1950.

Conran recorded:

> [there were four of us in the studio] producing designs for any rayon manufacturer who wanted them. If a client wanted flowers in a design we would order blooms not from any florist but from Constance Spry. We put on exhibitions – it was all lavishly done.

Although Conran was only with Lennon a few years, until 1952, he felt the job had helped him explore his talents more and to toughen him up for the realities of the textile industry. He was to produce designs for Liberty, Dunns of Bromley, Edinburgh Weavers and David Whitehead. A colleague at the time wrote of Conran:

> More of his textile designs have been put in production than any other young designer. In colours that range from the bold to the acidly delicious, they are extraordinarily sophisticated and elegant.

John Murray, of David Whitehead's, offered him a retainer of £1000 to produce designs. Although Conran worked on print designs for the firm, the directors got cold feet and decided against going ahead with them. Nevertheless with the income from Whitehead's, and with additional money invested in him by a mill owner, Conran took the opportunity to set up his own business – Conran Fabrics. At first it did its own printing but, as the business grew it was put out to specialist printing firms.

By then Conran was married and his wife, Shirley, began to design for the company which had started to attract lucrative commissions as from BEA, shipping companies and the like. Conran, now sure of himself, wrote a book *Printed Textile Design* which was used as a marketing tool by the company.

One might say Conran had got his feet on the textile ladder with the influence and support of Paolozzi; but they were more firmly placed by his being taken up by Lennon. Eventually, Conran's business talents and interests took his energies elsewhere, initially to furniture design, then to home furnishing and, alongside this to catering. But it was as a textile designer that he first made his name.

muriel pemberton

1909–1993

The name Muriel Pemberton is extremely unlikely to come to mind when considering the early careers of fashion designers. Yet her development was perhaps the most unique and certainly the most influential, at least when it came to the training of fashion designers if not to fashion design itself.

Pemberton , brought up in Burslem, came from a liberal home that positively encouraged artistic endeavours. Her father had a portrait photography business but was, himself, an amateur artist and an early experimenter with film. Her mother, an accomplished singer, was an original, if rather eccentric, needlewoman, making oftimes bizarre clothing for her four daughters. There were family theatrics, Pemberton contributing to the making of the costumes as well as the scenery.

Pemberton claimed she had wanted to be an artist from the age of five, but it was when she was fourteen, entirely on her own initiative, that she applied to the local art school, having seen a notice about an entrance examination. She marched in, took the exam, and won a three-year scholarship. Set on becoming an 'artist' she was ambitious, and her sights went beyond the Burslem School of Art to the Royal College of Art, for which she again gained a scholarship, starting there in 1928, aged nineteen.

She seems to have thrived in her first year at the College, which she devoted largely to drawing, but it was dawning on her that none of what she was learning was going to earn her a living. As she had followed in her mother's footsteps designing and making her own clothes, and as these were

Muriel Pemberton graduating from the Royal College of Art, 1931.

much admired by others, Pemberton considered the possibility of fashion designing. The major hurdle to this, she found, was that the Design School of the College did not offer a relevant course. The Head of the School was one, Professor Ernest Tristram, a rather remote man, a scholar of mediaeval murals, knowing nothing about fashion. Nevertheless when Pemberton approached him with her career problem he told her that if she could compile a good enough fashion design course for herself he would let her go ahead.

To prove it could be done, she did not just sit down with pen and paper to devise some hypothetical possibility, she acted. Firstly, through a contact, she got herself a weekly visit to the salon of a once royal couturier to sketch and to provide sketches for him. Then, turning to more basic matters, she drove a bargain with a school of cutting in Kensington whereby they would teach her cutting and she would teach design. Finally, to give context and academic stature to her studies, she approached the top man in the history of fashion, James Laver at the Victoria & Albert Museum, who, enchanted with her, provided her with lists of the essential reading on his subject. So armed, she confronted Tristram who, adequately impressed, gave her the go-ahead. She was to get the first Royal College Diploma in Fashion, which she herself had invented!

By the time Pemberton had finished her course she had set herself up with some part-time teaching of cutting and was giving private lessons in design. Realising she would need more work to keep herself independently she replied to an advertisement for someone to teach fashion illustration in the Graphics Department of St. Martins School of Art. Getting the job, her classes became so popular that the post was made full-time. By the time Pemberton had brought in cutters, dressmakers and milliners to help her, and added history of fashion, she had taken fashion out of Graphics and established it, with textiles, as a department in its own right, with students working on whole collections from concept to production, and with annual fashion shows that became a must-see for the industry. For Pemberton fashion drawing became a mere element in a full-blown fashion design course.

What Pemberton had done was to build on an art base, where previously any fashion design teaching that had existed at all had been built into dressmaking courses.

Her approach was anything but laying down the law – students were encourage to develop at their own pace and with their own inclinations. Bruce Oldfield and Bill Gibbs were two of the dozens of students who benefitted from her teaching, many becoming 'names' in the fashion design world; whilst Bernard Nevill, completing the circle, became Professor of Textiles at the Royal College. He was to write of her: 'A marvelous Midlands character, her basic kindness and niceness shining through everything.'

As her department grew Pemberton, inevitably, became more of an administrator but nevertheless continued to do some designing herself, mainly costumes for the theatre. Her design course was to morph into a standard course replicated at many other colleges in Britain and overseas. It had been in 1929 that the student had set about the task of educating herself; it was to be about twenty years later before the formidable Madge Garland set up the Fashion School at the Royal College of Art.

Right: St. Martins annual
student fashion show, undated.

jean muir

1928–1995

Jean Muir would have been rather uncomfortable at the thought of being included in a section on fashion designers for she never saw herself as such, and always referred to herself as a dressmaker. Born in London, but brought up in Bedford, she demonstrated an exceptional visual sensibility and practical skill from an early age – with drawing, embroidery and sewing completely absorbing the young Muir. At Dame Alice Harpur School in Bedford she had an inspiring art mistress, and before her teens could add to her practical talents a fairly wide appreciation of art, at least in terms of the 'old masters'.

However it never came to her mind to have a creative career, and, leaving school at seventeen, with only a modest school certificate, she took a number of clerical jobs in Bedford before coming to London in 1950. Later she was to write:

> I find it awfully difficult to pinpoint a moment in my life when my career started to take off. I didn't know what sort of career I wanted, so there was no sense in which I could plan it.

By chance Muir got a job as a junior in the stockroom serving the clothing department at Liberty's; she immediately felt she was in her spiritual home. She loved handling the materials, many of them of historic design. From the stock room she was moved to actually selling in the lingerie department, which would inevitably involve her doing

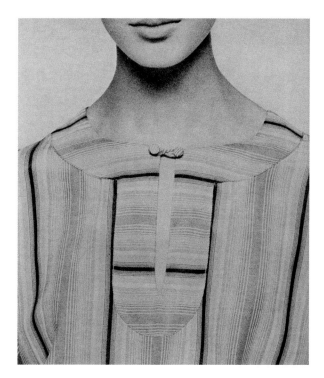

Muir dress design featured in *Vogue*, 1967.

some sketches for customers for those products that were, at that time, made-to-measure. Promoted to the Young Liberty department Muir was involved in fashion shows and was increasingly picking up knowledge of the fashion industry – from wholesale supplier to retailing – 'learning the business from A to Z' as she recorded it.

She decided to develop her own garment-making talents further, teaching herself to cut patterns, to discriminate between materials, and to design and make up more sophisticated clothes for herself (a useful facet as she was so small, barely five feet, that it was difficult to buy clothes that fitted). Muir decided to underpin all this with some evening classes – none seemed to offer more than she had already learnt about pattern cutting but she did attend classes at St. Martin's School of Art for fashion illustration, sometimes herself acting as model to supplement her modest Liberty wage.

After some six years at Liberty, and a short spell at Jacqmar, Muir joined Jaeger in 1956, by then in her late twenties. It is recorded she had a personal introduction, but there is no account of how she actually sold her self-taught know-how to them – what sort of folio she had accumulated. It

must have been quite impressive for she soon found herself designing a range of clothes for the company, having trips to Paris fashion shows as a perk. At Jaeger she was able to develop her design ideas, working with wool jersey and knitwear along with other daywear. So part and parcel of Jaeger had she become that it readily adopted her idea of having a Young Jaeger department.

Muir was to work at Jaeger until 1962, and although Liberty had given her inspiration, it was Jaeger that got her feet firmly on the design ladder, so firmly aided with an investment from a dress manufacturer, she felt able to leave, and to design a whole range of clothes under the label 'Jane & Jane'. By 1964 *Vogue* was hailing Muir as: 'one of the new young names that are giving the sixties an accent of their own'. By 1965, her reputation was such that she received one of the annual awards from the *Ambassador* magazine:

> …for applying the highest professional standards to British ready-to-wear which has made her an absolute authority among young fashion designers.

Opposite: Jean Muir evening dress design, 1968.

Above: Anthony Green's conception of Muir at work.

Soon after, in 1966, Muir set up her own business – Jean Muir Ltd. – with her husband as co-director. Although a gamble she saw it as gaining independence –'I can make my own style of clothes for better or worse'. Doing her own thing, with exemplary craftsmanship and a highly disciplined approach, brought success in the swinging sixties when, as she said, it was only too easy 'to put a sign on your door' and 'to get your name in the papers' without the time to learn the craft – 'fashion is not art, it is industry'. Muir was all about standards, whether she was targeting government agencies, educational establishments or the fashion industry itself in her critical comments.

Her own standards and independence from fashion trends, brought her a Royal Designer of Industry award in 1972, and a CBE in 1984. In 1980 she was given an exhibition in Leeds, the first in Britain to be devoted to the works of a living fashion designer.

In an obituary to her, Vogue listed her personality characteristics and style – 'perfectionist, purist, technician, integrity, craftsmanship' and 'pragmatist, perceptive, didactic, brave, crusader'.

marion foale

1939–

Foale was an Essex girl, brought up in a family which she described as having 'Victorian values'. She was educated at Ilford County High School for Girls, but having, herself, no desire to be 'respectable' or 'conventional', she found both home and school restraining. From her school days she had always seen herself as becoming a famous painter, and had begun to test her talents by entering competitions for young aspirants, winning, for example, a Blue Peter prize.

Although her parents, both working in the rag trade, had encouraged her practical interests (with her mother, a milliner, teaching her how to make her own clothes, and her father how to work a sewing machine), they were altogether less enthusiastic when 'practical' came to include 'artistic' and were strongly against her desire to go to art school. With the determination of a rather bolshy teenager, determined to do her own thing, Foale, by part-time work, funded her way through art school despite them.

Foale described her course at the South West Essex Technical College and School of Art (the latter in Walthamstow) as 'arts and crafts'. But Walthamstow Art School in the late 1950s and early '60s was in fact an exciting place, not stuck in the past – the tutors were young, barely out of college themselves, pop art and music had its sway – it was the time of Peter Blake, Ian Drury, Celia Birtwistle, and evening classes with Quentin Crisp as model. On her very first day Foale went down to the local pub at lunch time – she was going to be a free spirit.

The Queen's mantle designed by Foale when still a student.

She recalled: 'I went to be a painter, I didn't know fashion design even existed.'

By her second year she began to realize that painting was not going to earn her an income and discovered fashion. Her upbringing had given her the know-how of making a garment from start to finish, and this enabled her to skip a year and join the students on the fashion design course. Perhaps knowing so much about the practical side of garment making Foale saw the need to add the art aspect and particularly appreciated the life drawing classes, recording that that was where she learnt the most – presumably how the body is built, how it moves, and, therefore how it moves in clothes.

It was on the fashion course that Foale met Sally Tuffin and became part of a tight little clique of students, all of whom were to go on to study fashion at the Royal College of Art. They joined its Fashion School in 1959, run at the time by Janey Ironside. As so many design students were to report of their higher education studies, it was there Foale felt she learnt discipline, getting work done to standard and on time. The course still contained echoes of the 'finishing school' approach of its first Professor, Madge Garland (a concern for how the students presented themselves, for example, or the importance of attending the Paris fashion show, and so on). Foale described it all as 'deadly serious'. In spite of her 'bolshy' ways, she thrived at the College, and by her second year had been selected to submit designs for the Queen's mantel, worn at OBE ceremonies; it was her design that was chosen.

But concerned to design clothes that her generation would wear and not to supply middle-of-the-road safe designs for the trade, Foale, full of energy and confidence, wanted to get started. She was saved from the future she dreaded by a chance occurrence. Mary Quant and Alexander Plunkett-Green were asked to give a talk to the final year students. They had just opened Bazaar, and brought with them to the College the excitement of the King's Road. Foale immediately saw her escape route – 'if they can do it, we can!'

Iain Webb wrote 'America invented teenagers, Britain dressed them'; and that is what Foale and Tuffin set out to do. In 1961 Foale & Tuffin Ltd was established in a South Kensington flat. By 1962 they were selling to Woolland's young clothes buyer, on show in its windows, and were being featured in *Vogue*, making the clothes at home and delivering

Foale & Tuffin, Marlborough Court Boutique.

them by bus! By the mid-1960s the pair had a design team in operation, a wholesale business, and a building in Ganton Street (crossing Carnaby Street) along with some large contracts, as for J.C. Penny, the American department store chain.

Exactly who did what in the partnership is not recorded. There are hints that Tuffin was the talker and might thereby be assumed to have handled the transactions; but when, much later in her life, Foale started her own knitwear business she seems to have been more than competent on the commercial side. Certainly Foale pulled her weight when it came to the designing. When she was asked where she got her ideas from she replied: 'You didn't really get them from anywhere, you just see and then imbibe something without even realising.'

In 1972 Foale settled for family life in the country, but in the late '70s, concerned to add to the family income, she, independently, set up what was to become a thriving international knitwear business. In hindsight, the Quant/Plunkett Green talk may have shown Foale where the ladder lay, but it was the positive response from Woolands, with the resulting *Vogue* publicity, that got her feet firmly planted on it.

Winchester MS. Tenth Century MS. Foundational Hand

a test

a b c d e f g h i j k l m n o p q r s t u v w

O ALL YE WORKS
OF THE LORD
BLESS YE THE LORD:
PRAISE HIM AND
MAGNIFY HIM
FOR EVER

O ye Angels of the Lord,
bless ye the Lord: praise
him and magnify him for ever.
O ye Heavens, bless ye the
Lord: praise him & magni-
fy him for ever.

becoming a typographic or graphic designer

It was Richard Guyatt who claimed to have coined the term 'graphic design' when he was made Professor of the subject at the Royal College of Art in 1948. Whatever the source, graphic design as a profession is very much a twentieth century phenomenon, albeit it was still generally referred to as 'commercial' art well into the 1950s. Irrespective of name, the first half of the century brought a cornucopia of opportunities for the young would-be graphic designer – a largesse of riches.

Firstly, there was the exponential expansion of publishing, both of books and magazines. Although most publishers would not have afforded their own studio, they would have drawn on the artists employed by the plethora of advertising agencies and artists' studios coming into existence. Newspapers, at least the major national dailies, had largely been established before WWI, but magazines began to pour out from the presses, from less than three hundred before WWI to at least 1500 by the end of WWII. At least

Opposite: Edward Johnston's classroom blackboard used during his lectures, 1926.

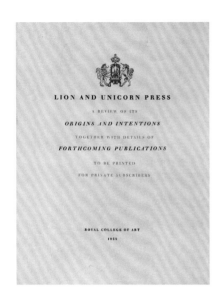

LION AND UNICORN PRESS

A REVIEW OF ITS

ORIGINS AND INTENTIONS

TOGETHER WITH DETAILS OF

FORTHCOMING PUBLICATIONS

TO BE PRINTED

FOR PRIVATE SUBSCRIBERS

ROYAL COLLEGE OF ART
1955

Above: An announcement regarding a Lion and Unicorn Press publication, 1955.

Opposite: Cover design for issue one of *Ark*, the RCA student magazine, 1950.

one hundred of these served women's interests, and, indeed, every specialist interest, society, region and organisation seemed to need their own publication, all such requiring typographic and graphic design to some extent.

Then there was the expansion of advertising and publicity, in the form of posters, press advertisements, brochures, leaflets and the like. Such personalities as Jack Beddington of Shell, Frank Pick of London Transport, Colin Anderson of the Orient Line, Stephen Tallents of the Empire Marketing Board and the General Post Office and William Teasdale of LNER, all became patrons of graphic designers, some commissioned when young and relatively untested. Although opportunities for young designers were prolific, few had the courage to go free-lance on leaving college but would tend to register with a studio where they would have to tackle very varied assignments, not all to their liking, but nevertheless adding usefully to their experience.

The newly fledged designers would have had numerous role models to give them encouragement to persevere in building their careers – a first wave included Edward McKnight Kauffer, Tom Purvis, Austin Cooper and Ashley Havinden; to be followed by a later generation, many Europeans settling in England, including F.H.K. Henrion, Hans Schleger, and Lewitt-Him, along with such homegrown ones as Tom Eckersley and Abram Games.

For the young becoming specifically interested in the typographic aspects of design, the twentieth century was to bring a

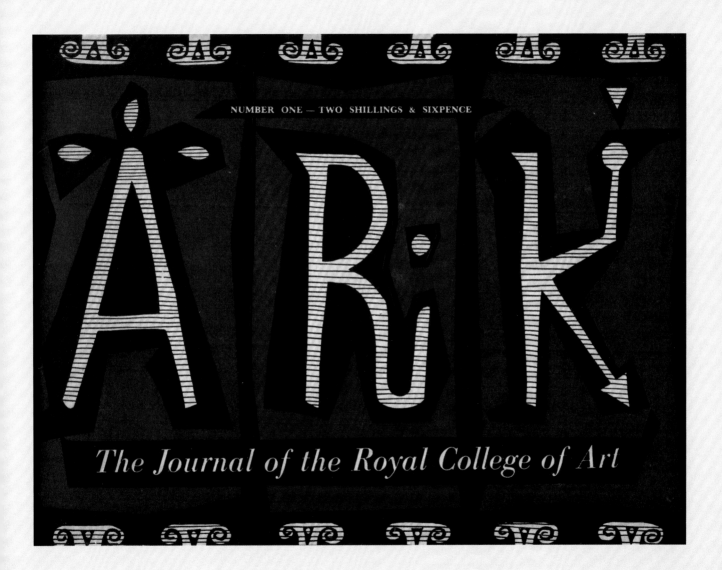

NUMBER ONE — TWO SHILLINGS & SIXPENCE

ARK

The Journal of the Royal College of Art

LONDON COUNTY COUNCIL

School of Photo-engraving and Lithography

6 BOLT COURT, FLEET STREET, E.C.4

PRINCIPAL ... A. J. BULL, M.Sc.

DAY AND EVENING CLASSES IN ALL PROCESS-REPRODUCTION METHODS

FOR ILLUSTRATION AND FOR COMMERCIAL ART

Line and Half-tone Block-making. Three and four colour blocks. Technical Photography. Photogravure (including the etching and proving of cylinders and plates). Photo-lithography (including offset proving). Lithography. Air brush work. Hand-engraving on wood.

Classes in drawing and design for reproduction including Life, Costume and Colour, and for design in relation to Book Decoration and Advertisement lay-out; also in hand-engraving on wood and in the preparation of originals for reproduction.

Lecture courses in Paper Making and Paper Testing.

A course of lectures on Photo-engraving methods and the general processes of reproduction is given by the Principal.

PROSPECTUSES CAN BE OBTAINED ON APPLICATION AT THE SCHOOL

renaissance in the art. Although the Europeans took the lead with their progressive type founderies and the Bauhaus teaching, in Britain Monotype awoke to new possibilities guided by Stanley Morison and fuelled by the evangelism of Beatrice Warde. Little journals, some rather short-lived, others as *Typographica* having a longer life, arrived to trumpet the cause of well-designed typography. Educationalists and role-models as Edward Johnston and Eric Gill, and a later generation including Jesse Collins and Herbert Spencer, all made art schools, and indeed, some schools of printing, aware of typography not only as a specialisation but as a profession in its own right. Publications, as the *Penrose Annual*, gradually began to show the interrelationship of printing, typography and graphic design so that young apprentices or art students could explore their interests and abilities across the range, not restricted by notional boundaries.

Educational establishments tried to keep up with the zeitgeist – courses labeled 'book production', rooted in arts and crafts and in wood-engraving, widened into a broader understanding of the potential of graphics. Graphics courses, when they arrived, became less snobbish about what had been considered the more vulgar end of the subject – advertising and publicity. Training for typographic design, which Beddington had complained about as abysmal, took longer to emerge, for printers' unions and confederations were reluctant for their apprentices to become contaminated with 'arty' matters, and were adamant

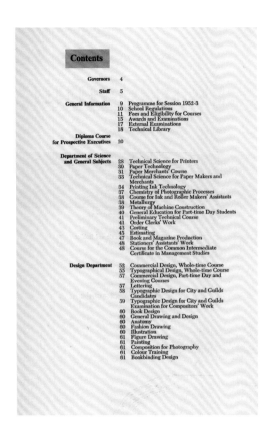

Above: The London College of Printing syllabus, from a publication released in 1953.

Right: The 'design' tower of the new building for the London College of Printing, 1962.

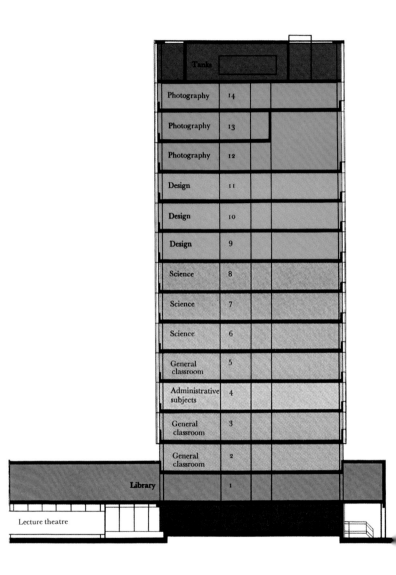

that art students should not get their hands anywhere near type or machinery. A symbolic breakthrough came when the London College of Printing allotted most of the floors of the tower in its new building at the Elephant & Castle to 'design'!

By the 1960s Herbert Spencer, the typographical evangelist, felt able, confidently, to declare that the typographer's rise in status to typographic designer was one of the key happenings in the printing world since the war. The budding typographic or graphic designer could not have been born at a more opportune time.

stanley morison

1889–1967

In 1912, a young bank clerk, aged twenty three, bought a copy of *The Times* newspaper from a stall in King's Cross Station; this apparently trivial happening was to change the life of Stanley Morison. Although others may be nominated as more original and prolific actual designers of type, Morison towers above the rest when it comes to influencing British typographic design in the first half of the twentieth century.

There was little in Morison's background to steer him in the direction of printing for a career. Born in Wanstead, he was brought up in north London. His father had been a clerk and then a commercial traveller, deserting his family when Morison was fifteen. Morison, who was brought up in Haringey, had attended the local elementary school where he gained a scholarship to the Brewer's Company School, but left as soon as possible, feeling it was necessary for him to start earning, given the family's circumstances.

There are, perhaps, in hindsight, a few slight threads to catch hold of, to predict Morison's future eminence in typography. Much of his years as a teenager were spent deciding where he stood in relation to religion, rather than what he might pursue as a career. From a non-conformist background, he went through a period of agnosticism, before, in 1908, he became a Catholic. It was as a Catholic that Morison first became aware of the beauty of exceptional printing, that to be found in early religious books and tracts, particularly in volumes of plainchant. This led him to extend his knowledge

Drawing of Morison by Frances Macdonald, 1939.

by visits to the British Museum to look at early printed books.

By the fateful day of his purchase of *The Times*, Morison had worked some seven years at the London City Mission, and then at the London branch of the French bank Societe Generale. The particular issue of the significant newspaper bought, contained a supplement on print. Morison was enthralled, describing it as 'spectacular', and on such a slight whim, stimulated by the articles on calligraphy, private presses and printing, he decided to study typography and type design.

But the supplement not only contained, for Morison, exciting articles, but carried an advertisement for a forthcoming journal launch – *The Imprint*, which the now enthusiastic young bank clerk rushed to buy, its first issue published in 1913. The journal, aiming to raise the standard of British printing, was published from 11 Henrietta Street in Covent Garden. This first issue carried an advertisement for an editorial assistant: 'a young man of good education with experience of publishing and advertising'. Morison had neither of these, but that did not deter him, and, on applying, managed to convince the publisher, Gerald Meynell, that he was

ABCDEFGHIJKLMNOPQ
abcdefghijklmnopqrstuvwxyz
ABCDEFGHIJKLMNOPQ
abcdefghijklmnopqrstuvwxyz
£1234567890

best suited for the post. His religious conversion may well have helped as the Meynell's were a well-known Catholic family.

Although *The Imprint* had a rather short life, Gerald Meynell introduced the young Morison to his uncle Wilfred, the managing director of the Catholic publishing firm Burns & Oates. Wilfred's son Francis, only twenty-one, was in charge of the firm's book design, and Morison became his assistant. The two young men began their partnership working on books together. Morison got drawn into a printing network including such personalities as B.H. Newdigate (the scholar-printer) and Eric Gill (the future type designer). Francis Meynell wrote of his closeness to Morison: 'We shared a devotion to religion, to socialist politics, to the seventeenth century Fell types and to cricket'.

Morison wrote of his developing attitude to the role of the typographer, the one he would adopt:

It is not for the printer to assess the literary value of a text. Clearness in printing makes demands upon the printer's intelligence

rather than his emotions, upon conscientiousness rather than enthusiasm.

Largely concerned, as he would be, with legibility and getting the meaning of a text across simply, this inevitably became a matter of aesthetics, of design.

When Meynell started The Pelican Press (to produce well-designed material for the Socialist cause), he was also working for *The Daily Herald*, and he asked Morison to take over the responsibility for the Press. Morison by then felt sufficiently confident to write on his chosen career, publishing

The Craft of Printing in 1921, to be followed in the years ahead by a prolific outflow of articles and books. When Meynell returned to run The Pelican Press, Morison took a job with Charles Hobson, a Manchester advertising agent who was starting the Cloister Press. Hobson wrote:

> My object was to lift him out of Fleet Street and transplant him in a daisy-sprinkled meadow at Heaton Mersey, some six miles south of Manchester. It was there I had planned to build the Cloister Press. And it

Below: Single sheet prospectus
for Morison's classic text, *First
Principles of Typography*, 1936.

FIRST PRINCIPLES
OF
TYPOGRAPHY

BY

STANLEY MORISON

Printing is multiplication
Type must be familiar
Composition and Imposition
Principles of Composition
The use of leading
Proportions of the page
Page and chapter headings
The title-page
The dictates of Commerce
The preliminaries
So-called fine printing

From all booksellers. 2s. 6d. net

CAMBRIDGE UNIVERSITY
PRESS

was Morison I wanted to help the composing room in the good cause of the 'P's' and 'Q's', to give each page a happy face, in short to be Master of Good Manners in this new and better Printing house.

Morison was also to be involved, with Oliver Simon, on a new typographical journal *The Fleuron*, as well as the *Penrose Annual*, a yearbook of progress in printing and the graphic arts published by the printers Percy Lund Humphries.

But neither Manchester nor Hobson suited Morison and he persuaded Hobson to open a London office so that he could return to home ground. By 1922 the new Cloister Press was experiencing financial difficulties and Morison decided to start to work as a freelance typographical consultant. Already working as typographical adviser to the University of Cambridge Press, it was then that Morison approached the Lawton Monotype organisation. For more than forty years Morison was to act as consultant to Monotype. He got the company to realise the profitability in cutting new type, commissioning new ones, as Gill Sans. As typographical consultant to *The Times*, instigating

Times New Roman in 1932, having rounded the circle as it were, by writing an article for a *Times* supplement about newspaper types. He wrote of the new Times type:

> The new types proposed for *The Times* will tend towards the 'modern' though the body of the letter will be more or less old-face in appearance.

Beatrice Warde, who was his colleague for some forty years at Monotype, and with whom he worked producing the *Monotype Recorder*, wrote of Morison's influence on people:

> …their minds expanded to him as greedily as tired lungs rise to the wind from an April forest whipping into a stuffy room.

Less poetically, she evaluated his contribution to typography:

> …an inventive designer and profoundly influential practitioner, whose anonymous hand has been behind a whole series of revolutions and reforms affecting the look of the visible word in both hemispheres.

Morison declined a CBE and a knighthood when they were offered, but was elected a Royal Designer for Industry in 1960, an award given for his influence on British typography. It is generally considered that he had taught himself his trade and its history more comprehensively than if he had attended any course; and, in his turn, he became a major educator (by his writing and lecturing) and influencer (as a role model and patron) of generations of would-be young typographic designers – but it all started with the purchase of *The Times*.

ruari mclean

1917–2006

As with a number of other typographic design-ers, as a child words meant more to McLean than images. He came from a middle class home and was privately educated, his preparatory school The Dragon, in Oxford, his public school Eastbourne College, where he boarded.

Born in Scotland, the family settled in Oxford where his father worked in Customs and Excise. Both parents had been university educated, his mother reading history at Edinburgh, his father studying at Imperial College. Although McLean's father had chosen a career in the Civil Service, his home interests were artistic and practical – drawing and painting, modeling, calligraphy, and photogra-phy. He does not seem to have actively shared any of these with his son, but, nevertheless, there would have been a home atmosphere of creativity. Ruari McLean did show some interest in art at school, but found writing easier. He wrote of his prefer-ence: 'words, it didn't seem to matter much what they meant, were intoxicating to me'.

From Eastbourne College, McLean had tried and failed to get a classical scholarship to Oxford, and was left, at eighteen, with no clear thoughts as to what to do next. The local government Careers Service used to have an in-joke that if someone was good at religious studies and carpentry they should be advised to become an undertaker. Much along these lines, when McLean's mother turned to her friend Basil Blackwell for advice, Blackwell said that the boy could draw and liked reading so he should consider printing.

Linocut by Ruari McLean, 1936.

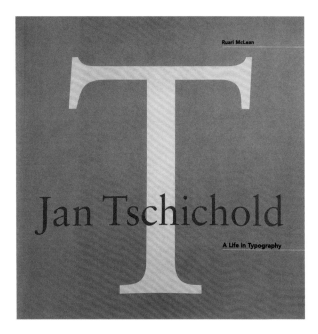

The book cover for Ruari McLean's biography of Jan Tschichold, 1997.

Luckily for McLean, Blackwell not only ran a bookshop but also had a publishing and a printing business, and offered the young McLean the opportunity to spend some months at the Shakespeare Head Press, which Blackwell had recently brought. The Press not only operated as a general printers, but specialised in the designing and printing of fine, limited edition books that other publishers put its way.

The Press, run by Bernard Newdigate, did its composition by hand and there McLean got to do a little type-setting. Yet it was something altogether more incidental that was to stir the young McLean:

[I] noticed a writing I had not seen before and rather liked. It was my first sight of an italic hand; the letter was from Stanley Morison [of whom I had never heard] to Bernard Newdigate. My real education was beginning.

After a few months with the Press, McLean made an exchange trip to Germany, where he took a short language course and spent a brief period with the Weiner Press. By the time he returned

An example of Ruari McLean's work with Marcus Morris on the *Eagle* comic, 1954.

to England he had decided printing was for him and that he should take it seriously. This led to his enrolling on a one year course at the Edinburgh School of Printing, emerging with a City & Guild certificate. It was a course actually meant for part-time apprentices, not geared to full-time students, which suggests that McLean was, by now, taking charge of his own education. He recorded that:

> ...the best part of the school for me was a collection of pages or books by Gutenberg, Fustand Schoeffer, Jensen, Aldus Manutius, Estienne, Tory, Plantin, and so on...

And, on his own initiative, he appears to have spent a good deal of time in the Advocates Library, reading up on Updike, Morison and articles in the journal *The Fleuron*.

McLean described his time in Edinburgh as 'a valuable growing up year'. He followed this by a further year working at Waterlow & Son in Dunstable, a large and modern printers in comparison to the Shakespeare Head. The Shakespeare Head, the Edinburgh course and then Waterlow's, in retrospect, seem to have provided a kind of self-organised apprenticeship. McLean was then able to add to this a period working with Newdigate on a commission from The Studio for Newdigate's book *The Art of the Book*. For this McLean actually produced his first designs, for the cloth binding and jacket. He also got involved with some work for The Studio's *Year Book of Decorative Art*, but when the Newdigate book was finished McLean was let go.

He approached Penguin Books to see whether they had a vacancy for a would-be typographer. Although there was not one at the time, Penguin's production manager, Edward Young, invited him to share a flat. This was not actually what McLean was seeking then, but, in fact, by agreeing to share, he was brought into contact with the printing side of the publishing world socially. Instead of Penguin he found himself working on advertisements as a trainee art director at the agency J. Walter Thompson. But he did not feel at home in the advertising world and yet again made a change, joining Lund Humphries in Bradford, in 1939, as 'assistant manager composing room'.

As McLean had stumbled on Morison at the Shakespeare Head, at Lund Humphries he

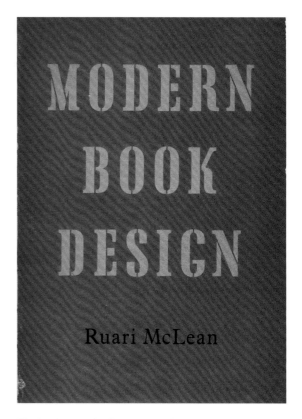

The book cover for Ruari McLean's classic text *Modern Book Design*, 1958.

came upon some typographical examples of Jan Tschichold, for whom the printers had just mounted an exhibition in London. He was so excited by these to the extent that he immediately wrote to Tschichold in Switzerland and went out to see him – it was 1939 and he was twenty-two. McLean had spent some four years since leaving school, flitting here and there as a 'learner', as he refered to himself, and any attempt to consolidate his learning was now to be frustrated by the onset of war – McLean's career was on hold.

His war service, with Naval Intelligence, took him to the Far East and then back to Oxford; 1945 found him back at J. Walter Thompson. It was then that he re-applied to Penguin, was accepted, and began to take up the challenge of typographical design, working on the Puffin Picture Books and Penguin's Progress, the company's publicity booklet. Penguin had brought Tschichold over to oversee its printing standards, and, by chance, McLean's office was next door to that of his 'guru', so much time was spent sitting at the feet of the master.

At last, aged twenty nine, McLean could feel he was breaking free of his printing chrysalis stage. With increasing confidence, commissions passed to him from a friend and some teaching at the Royal College of Art, he decided to try to operate freelance. And then came a breakthrough. Having helped a local vicar with his parish magazine he was approached by another cleric, one Marcus Morris, who was about to publish a 'christian' comic. The rest is history! McLean was soon involved as typographical advisor to what morphed into *The Eagle*, then, in addition, *The Robin*, *The Girl* and all the spin-offs of annuals, ephemera and so on.

There followed a highly successful partnership with a colleague, forming Rainbird McLean (seven years with some forty clients handling some seventy books) and, as 'the grand old man' of typography, receiving a CBE and being appointed Typographic Adviser to her Majesty's Government at HMSO.

anthony froshaug

1920–1984

Anthony Froshaug, a leading exponent, as a designer and teacher, of 'modern' typography, claimed to have decided on his future career in his early teens:

> I came to design from a childhood inter-
> est in producing carbon-papered, later
> gelatined-copied, later squeeze-screened
> and later duplicated newsheets at home and
> at early school…I was in love with math-
> ematics and astronomy and map-making
> and letter forms and Whittaker's Almanac;
> visual shorthand and annotations came
> early, but I do not think I could ever
> 'draw'…from the age of fourteen I knew I
> wanted to…earn my living as a designer.

Born in Little Stanmore, his family were comfort-ably off, his Norwegian father being Director of Norwegian Railways, working from its London office. Froshaug was sent to board at a typical British public school, Charterhouse, in Godalming. Although he loved the mathematics classes and gained matriculation, he 'walked out' at seventeen, rejecting the school and all it stood for, with no intention of studying for university entrance and every intention of going to art school.

Froshaug started on an illustration and book production course at the Central School of Arts & Crafts, but was fairly dismissive of his time there:

> I do not think that what I actually learned
> at Central, in terms of technique or skills,

was very important; the most important was in being in contact with people like John Farleigh, Morris Kestleman and Jesse Collins, and in working in a free co-educational atmosphere … my interest in design became more and more specific – from posters and book jackets (the only design projects we ever did), concentrating more and more on letter forms and lettering. I was fascinated by typography.

Froshaug, studying at Central from 1937 to 1939, has been described as a wayward and obstinate student, refusing to do life drawing, and never seriously seeming to be studying anything, obsessed only by lettering and layout. His enthusiasm for these was described as 'infectious', his fellow students gaining something from his delight.

Any career plans he may have had were interrupted by call up for the war. Froshaug's stand was anarchic rather than pacific in relation to this, and by registering for a medical degree, thus avoiding military service, he managed to see through the war partly studying and partly working on a few typographical commissions that came his way. Some of these came through his father, as one designing statistical charts for the Norwegian Manpower Board.

It was during the war that Froshaug started Isomorph, a publishing enterprise aiming to produce monthly reprints of original scientific texts, not for the masses but to be bought by subscription, combining his interests in science and in print production. His coming upon a book by the Swiss typographer Jan Tschichold, and the lengthy and abortive attempts to publish translations of his writings, only contributed, along with other factors, to the whole enterprise collapsing. Nevertheless the project enabled him to become thoroughly familiar with Tschichold's approach and his writing. Robin Kinross, Froshaug's biographer wrote that:

> By the late 1940s he had thoroughly absorbed the lessons of Jan Tschichold, circa 1935, and was becoming, in my view the designer who best understood and developed Tschichold's new typography.

This he would not only have practiced himself but proselytized to students, colleagues, and anyone open to such modernism.

Top: Portrait of Anthony Froshaug.

Above: Guido Morris, Froshaug's guru.

It was when Froshaug, on a break to Cornwall in 1946, met up with Guido Morris (the self-declared master printer) and touched type for the first time, that his career got a jolt forward:

> I had never, at art school, been allowed to touch type (I once went into the room capitalised TYPOGRAPHY and saw J.H. Mason poised on his high clicker-stool, who ordered me out).

Froshaug was to write to Morris:

> Just to handle type; that was the unintended education you gave me … I was corrected by your devotion to the idea of typesesetting, of printing and paper … You were the first person I ever met who had a library of books, of real books.

The results of this meeting led Froshaug to set himself up as a jobbing printer in Cornwall, with the financial support gained from some London commissions from the St. George's Gallery and the Institute of Contemporary Art. In seeking

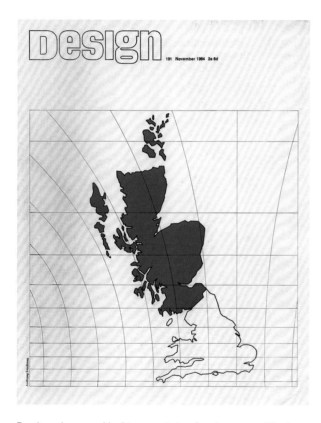

Froshaug honoured by his commission for the cover of *Design* magazine (an issue on Scottish design), 1964.

commissions he described himself as 'printer and free-lance typographer'; as an eccentric modernist he became his own compositor. Paul Stiff wrote of these years:

> … one senses each job being a new project, the chance of an exploration in configuring language, playing down the type while playing up its spatial disposition.

Froshaug's work in Cornwall was interrupted by a short time teaching at Central, persuaded to do so by Jesse Collins. Although this gave him some insight into his possible enjoyment of the teaching role, he was not approved of in his probationary year as: 'failing to secure that degree of confidence and co-operation from technical staff which is one of the essentials of the position'.

Froshaug's personality probably did not help in dealing tactfully with the inbuilt conflict between those concerned with the education of trade students and those teaching typographic and graphic design.

During his Cornish printing period Froshaug organised a further learning experience, with a tour

An example of Froshaug's
approach to typographic
design, as seen is his layout for
an ICA pamphlet, 1948.

The Institute of Contemporary Arts **ICA**

Managing Committee	Herbert Read (*Chairman*) Edward Clark E C Gregory Roland Penrose Peter Watson
Advisory Committee	Peggy Ashcroft Frederick Ashton J B Brunius Alex Comfort Michel St Denis Geoffrey Grigson Arthur Jeffress G M Hoellering Frederick Laws Robert Melville E L T Mesens J M Richards
Director	Ewan Phillips

Policy & Aims
The Institute of Contemporary Arts has been founded by a Committee representing the various branches of the arts. In due course, as its activities increase, it will take premises or plan for itself a building, which will allow scope for all the arts to meet under one roof

Co-operative
It will gather together & co-ordinate the arts of our time and establish a common ground for a progressive movement. It will provide club facilities where members can meet together in an informal way for purposes of discussion. Artists will thus be brought into contact with each other and with their public

Creative & Experimental
It will undertake exhibitions, performances & other activities without depending on commercial standards. It will enable artists of all kinds to join in search of new forms of expression and will encourage the development of modern techniques

Informative
It will establish contacts on a wide international basis and will set up a library and centre of information relating to contemporary developments in the arts in all countries

For further information write or telephone
The Director, The Institute of Contemporary Arts, 6 Fitzroy Street, London W1. MUSeum 5145

Achievements 1948 / 1949

February	The ICA began its first public activities in February 1948.
March	Exhibition *40 Years of Modern Art, a Selection from British Collections*. Held at the Academy Hall, Oxford Street, London W1 for four weeks. Over 20,000 people visited this exhibition. During the exhibition two concerts of *Contemporary Chamber Music* were held, including first performances of works by Luigi Dallapiccola, Alban Berg, Igor Stravinsky & Alan Bush; also two *Poetry Readings* at which T S Eliot, Louis MacNeice, C Day Lewis, Dylan Thomas, Eugenio Montale & Alberto Moravia, among others, read from their own works
April	A third *Poetry Reading* was held on W H Auden's arrival in London, at which he read from his own works
August	Two free lectures on *Modern Architecture* were given by Professor Giedion of Switzerland, in conjunction with the Mars Group
October	A special gala première of the Italian film *Paisa* was given in aid of the Institute by the generosity of the Academy Cinema

Membership Form

I, Insert:
Full name _____
State _____ Mr Mrs Miss
Address _____
wish to become a member of the ICA and enclose cheque A B C D E

Usual Signature _____

Deed of Covenant

I, Insert:
Full name _____
State _____ Mr Mrs Miss
Address _____
hereby covenant with Living Arts Ltd, that I will during the term of seven years from or during my life (whichever period shall be shorter) pay to the said Society each year such a sum as will after deduction of Income-Tax at the current rate amount to the sum of guineas from my general fund of taxed income so that I shall receive no personal or private benefit from the said annual payments.
In witness whereof I have hereunto set my hand and seal
this day of one thousand nine hundred & forty

Date _____
Appropriate _____
Amount _____

Signed, sealed & delivered by the above-named

Date _____

Usual Signature _____

in the presence of

Signature _____
Address _____
Occupation _____
Signature _____
Address _____
Occupation _____

Terms of Membership
The first 2000 members will be exempted from any entrance fee. Membership subscriptions are as follows

Annual	A 2 guineas yearly – or B 1½ guineas yearly by Deed of Covenant for 7 years C 15 shillings yearly student's membership
Foundation	D 100 guineas for life – or E 10 guineas yearly by Deed of Covenant for 7 years

Address form to ICA, 6 Fitzroy Street, London W1 →

Subscription by Deed of Covenant
The Institute of Contemporary Arts is incorporated under Living Arts Limited, 24 Coleman Street, London EC2, a non-profit-making body registered under The Companies' Act, 1929. (Registered number X76796A)
If any member signs a Deed of Covenant, the Institute can reclaim the Income Tax which has been paid on the subscription. In this way, with no additional cost to themselves, members can considerably increase the income of the Institute. For example, a member paying 1½ guineas yearly and signing the Deed of Covenant *overleaf* enables a further £1 5s 9d to be claimed from the Inland Revenue. Similarly, the subscription of 10 guineas (or more, should the member so desire) yearly, by Deed of Covenant, will be worth £19 1s 8d to the Institute
Cheques should be made payable to: *Living Arts Limited*

Address form to ICA, 6 Fitzroy Street, London W1 →

across France, Switzerland and Italy, visiting printers on the way. It was when he was in Zurich that he met Max Bill with whom he had previously been in contact when seeking works for Isomorph to publish. Some years later when Bill was establishing a new design school in Ulm – the Hochschule für Gestaltung (HSG) – he asked Froshaug to come to teach there. Possibly motivated by the fact that he would be teaching at a higher level than he had done at Central, and would have a free hand to experiment with European modernism, he accepted. It was at Ulm that Froshaug was converted to taking the role of teacher, with a preference for running atelier workshop style student groups rather than anything didactic. Kinross wrote of Froshaug's approach to teaching:

> …he was egalitarian, conversational, informal, and against all mystification. His authority was not a matter of force or will. The situation was rather that of a journey made in common with the students…

His outspoken, rather abrasive style, ranging widely and wildly in what he chose to talk about, 'a free spirit' as he has been described, seems to have appealed to his students with whom he would tend to socialise out of class time.

There followed teaching spells at the Royal College of Art, the School of Art at Watford College of Technology, back to Central, and finally at the London College of Printing. Watford rewarded him, in 1965, with an exhibition of some twenty years of his printing work. He was also to be one of the first to adopt and to experiment with digital typography.

Although Froshaug might be said to have been more effective as a starter of projects than as a completer or stayer, he was part of the brilliant post-war cohort of typographers bringing modernism to British printing, albeit he could be described as a maverick on the fringe. Although his career could be said to have started with Jesse Collins seeing him as a potential teacher, and with Guido Morris adopting him for a short time as a kind of apprentice, Froshaug saw his whole career as continuously that of a learner.

ashley havinden

1903–1973

Ashley Havinden, generally referred to as Ashley, his signature to his works, was born in Maidstone, Kent, one of six children. His mother died when he was nine. His father, a wine merchant, was very much in charge of his upbringing, persuading Christ's Hospital, in Horsham, to give the boy a free place, and putting his foot down when Ashley declared his intention of becoming an artist.

Christ's Hospital seems to have achieved little in its attempt to educate Ashley for he left the school without formal educational qualifications. His father considered advertising an altogether more remunerative path for him to take than art, but appears to have seen training in printing as a good basis before entering the advertising world. Ashley was employed as a trainee at Waterlow & Langton, and then at Sun Engraving, both in Watford and both well-established companies with good reputations. Ashley would certainly have picked up useful know-how of lithographic and photogravure printing in the eighteen months or so he was employed with them, but he expressed himself as bored, possibly finding the routine jobs he would have been allotted, as lacking in stimulation, insufficiently testing his talents.

Ashley's father, as luck would have it, knew one, William Crawford, who had set up his advertising agency in 1914, and who, by his dynamism, was to build it into one of the leading agencies in Britain in the first half of the twentieth century. Again it was possibly due to his father's persuasive style of operating, that Ashley, a raw, unqualified

SHE *Husbands are nearly as difficult to choose as silk stockings!*
HE *Ah, but you can't expect absolute perfection in a mere man.*

KAYSER STOCKINGS are a sheer joy to look at and to wear. Pure silk – glimmering and satin-smooth. Pure unweighted dyes that keep their delicate tints through washing after washing.
Their loveliness is protected by cunning workmanship; by the famous ladder-preventing 'Marvelstripe' which, in deference to our short skirts, now appears above instead of below the knee.
See how intricately the foot and seams of a Kayser stocking are tailored to lie smoothly along the difficult curves of knee and ankle. This 'full-fashioning' of Kayser stockings means that they give with every movement, yet never lose their lovely line.

full-fashioned ***Kayser*** *thread silk*

STOCKINGS

Press Advertisement Designed by Ashley

youth, joined the agency in 1922, as a trainee on £1 a week.

Crawford's was to provide all the stimulation and encouragement that Ashley had found lacking at the printing works. Not only was he fortunate to have found a personality as Crawford to support him and provide him with the challenges and the freedom to develop what talents he had, but to find himself with two outstanding colleagues as Saxon Mills, copywriter, and Margaret Sangster, account executive, the trio to become a formidable force in the industry. The role of Margaret Sangster in Ashley's development should not be underestimated for not only did she bring in and steer the progress of many of the commissions he undertook, but she married him, thus providing both work and domestic support.

On joining Crawford's Ashley was given a position as trainee layout and typography artist and illustrator. It was in the first two of these roles that he was to find his true métier for he was never to prove a strong illustrator in spite of it being part of his remit. Within a very few years he was working on major accounts as those for Chrysler Motors and Eno's Fruit Salts. Such was Crawford's attitude to giving youth its head, that, by 1929, when he was twenty six, Ashley was made Art Director of the agency; by 1930 his work was being featured in *Modern Publicity*, the annual which showcased the best of a year's graphic designs.

When it came to typography and layout Ashley was particularly influenced by what was going on at the Bauhaus in Germany, and, in England, by the activities of Francis Meynell, Harold Curwen and Stanley Morison. He had met Morison in 1924, and it was Morison who encouraged him to contribute to trying to improve the general standard of typographic and graphic design. In 1926 Ashley had accompanied Crawford on a fact-finding tour of progressive German type foundries, as Gebruder Klingspor and the Bayner Type Foundry; and it was in that year that Morison commissioned him to produce an entirely new type face to be named 'Ashley Crawford'. Morison wrote of the time:

> Things were done to type arrangements in the Crawford Camp, which had certainly never been dreamt of before... The Crawford Camp showed courage and

Ashley's advertisement for Basildon Bond notepaper.

90

imagination and greatly widened the possible ways of using a given newspaper space. They were responsible for new techniques in illustration and the encouragement of many new types, both native and foreign.

F.H.K. Henrion, a major graphic designer of the mid-twentieth century, wrote of Ashley:

> …he would go to any length to learn what other artists and designers had done, to improve his mind and performances, as he had an almost childlike belief in the ultimate salvation of the world by design.

And, indeed, in the 1930s Ashley met up with many of the well-known architects, artists and designers of the time, many becoming his friends, including Moholy Nagy, Herbert Beyer, McKnight Kauffer and Walter Gropius. As well as becoming a major player when it came to the graphic arts, Ashley also designed textiles and rugs as well as continuing to paint, his original ambition. But it was joining Crawford's (where he remained for the rest of his working life), that was to set his foot on the ladder.

Ashley Script typeface for Monotype (*Ark*, 1955 advertisement).

tom eckersley

1914–1997

Tom Eckersley became a major graphic designer in the middle years of the twentieth century. Paul Rennie, his biographer, considers that his influence cannot be overstated, not only by the impact that his own strong designing style had on the profession, but by his pioneering work as an educationalist.

Eckersley had a rural upbringing on his father's farm on the outskirts of Manchester. His father had wanted to become a Methodist minister, and although this did not prove practical, much of his life was spent as a lay preacher. He was a bookish man, and when not farming or preaching would spend his time browsing the secondhand bookshops of Manchester; the house was crammed with books.

Eckersley was a 'delicate' child, succumbing to whatever ailment was endemic at the time. Much of his early life was spent away from school, reading and drawing, as a form of occupational therapy. The farm was financially fragile and his parents considered he should have a more secure career than working with his father, and considered some kind of office work; Eckersley was to follow what was thought to be an appropriate course at Lord's Commercial College in Bolton. But his mother, a woman of considerable culture, could see his heart was not in clerical affairs, and, noticing a feature in a local paper about an art school, suggested that this might be a more satisfactory alternative. At the age of sixteen, Eckersley was registered as a student at Salford School of Art.

Eckersley Lombers design as featured in *Commercial Art* magazine, 1935.

Eckersley's time at Salford was crucial to his development as a designer. Firstly it widened his horizon by introducing him to 'modernism', with hung illustrations of European artists and designers along its corridors, and related magazines as *Cahiers d'Art* and *Gebrauchsgraphik* in its library. Then it helped him build confidence in his ability with the stimulating teaching of the staff, particularly that of Martin Tyas. In 1934 he won the School's Heywood Medal for best student (albeit out of only about twenty) and this certainly made him more sure of the direction he should take. And, crucial to his early years as a designer, he formed a close friendship with a fellow student, Eric Lombers. It is possible that the two began to consider themselves as something special, apart from the other students, for, even whilst at art school, they pushed their tables together and worked in combination. It was the strength of this coupling that perhaps determined them to develop their careers as free-lancers, which few students did, or, indeed, could afford to do, immediately on leaving college.

But then they were supported in their venture by the benign interest of the School's Principal,

Presents for Men — just a part

of the Austin Reed service

Left: Eckersley Lombers poster for Austin Reed, 1938.

Opposite: Eckersley Lombers poster for London Transport Board, c. 1940.

Harold Rhodes. Rhodes had come to Salford from the Royal College of Art, was actively interested in design, and a member of the Design and Industries Association. It was Rhodes who encouraged the pair, who were only finding the odd job in Manchester and Liverpool, to go to London; and it was Rhodes who was to provide them with an 'open sesame' key – an introduction to Frank Pick of London Transport.

In fact life in London initially proved hard for the pair, settling in two rooms in Ebury Street, near Victoria Station, in 1934. Eckersley's parents were funding him modestly and cautioned that aiming to become free-lance so soon after leaving art school

was over-ambitious. And, indeed, for some weeks they touted their work around unsuccessfully. Eckersley appears to have been the spokesman, and applied himself energetically, for by 1935 Lombers-Eckersley were allotted some four pages in *Commercial Art*, the main graphics journal of the time, which showed examples of their work, including a full-page coloured design and some half dozen black and white sketches.

The article, described them as 'on the threshold of their careers', noting that they had only recently finished at art school, and praising them for the economy of their design, their versatility and originality. The confidence of youth comes across in

BY BUS TO THE PICTURES TO-NIGHT

ECKERSLEY LOMBERS

35-4716-1,000-D·P·C

their publicity: 'Our ambition is to strive to uphold the standard of commercial art that certain other artists have so gallantly raised.'

'Certain other artists' very definitely included Cassandre, an important influence. And yet again, in 1935, Eckersley-Lombers were given pages in *Commercial Art*, this time Eckersley giving an account of their efforts trying to get work in London. He described their frustration, as free-lancers, trying to get commissions from advertising agencies, which, in turning them down, advised them to join a commercial studio. He tells of how persistence paid off with commissions from newspapers and from the Nickeloid Electrotype Co., which gave them virtually a free hand in what they were asked to do. In 1941, after the pair had virtually broken up, the journal described them as being responsible for 'some of the most vital and interesting advertising work of the day'.

But their early London commissions were minnows compared to the response the two got when taking up Rhodes introduction to Frank Pick. He agreed to see their portfolio, and invited them to meet his publicity manager, Christian Barman. The rest is history, for this first visit produced a

Tom Eckersley poster design for the British Omnibus Company, 1970s.

constant flow of commissions, through to the onset of war. Barman wrote of them:

> They have a knack of simplifying a problem and presenting the salient necessities with an arresting boldness, their colouring is rich and very personal and they are masters of the use of large masses of graded colour.

Along with Eckersley's association with the Post Office, which began in 1938 (and was to last through to the 1960s), Eckersley's feet were not only on the career ladder but very firmly so.

Eckersley was to become one of the major poster designers of the mid-century years – his style modernist, with strong colours, the flattest and simplest of imagery, and sharply defined outlines. The onset of war was to break up the partnership, with each of the pair enlisting in different Services. After the war ended Eckersley was to build up an impressive career for himself with long lasting working relationships, not only with the Post Office but with the Royal Society for the Prevention of Accidents.

Eckersley was to influence the graphics scene not only by the strength and individuality of his style but by his teaching. Although he, himself, had never seriously considered full-time teaching he was invited to join the staff of the London College of Printing in 1954, becoming Head of Design in 1957, and staying there for some twenty years. His nonconformist progressive background led him to feel free to tread his own path – to build up an international team of tutors, to ensure that 'design' was key to the College's operating on its new site, and to build up an ethos of design as problem solving, the studio as an experimental laboratory. All this within the atmosphere of the left-leaning counter culture that was the zeitgeist from the 1960s onwards.

alan fletcher

1931–2006

Although many columns have been penned lauding Alan Fletcher – 'the most influential figure', 'the most highly regarded', 'producer of the most iconic design', 'the godfather of graphic design' – and much more of the same, little is recorded of his early life before he joined the Mount Olympus of graphic designers.

That he happened to be born in Nairobi where his father was a civil servant, seems an irrelevance, for Fletcher's father died when he was five, and he was brought up by his grandparents in London. The onset of WWII saw him evacuated to Christ's Hospital School in Horsham. This was a school grooming its pupils for the army, the church or the city, none of which interested him to pursue as a career.

Fletcher showed an early talent for drawing, and, on leaving school, aged eighteen, he enrolled on an illustration course at Hammersmith School of Art. With no family background in the arts, the year there must have bought him some time to find out more about where his own talents lay and how he could advance his art education in London. He went on to study at the Central School of Arts and Crafts in the heady days of the 1950s, where he was not only taught by such inspiring staff as Anthony Fraushag, but was of the remarkable student generation that included Derek Birdsall, Ken Garland, and Colin Forbes. In hindsight the friendships Fletcher built there seem more significant as contributors to his future than the content of what he was studying, for Colin Forbes was to become a

FIGURE PAINTING

do you need a book?

ZWEMMERS ART BOOKSHOP 76/80 Charing Cross Road London WC2 Telephone Temple Bar 4710

Far left: Fletcher as a student at the Royal College of Art, 1950s.

Left: Fletcher in his English whimsy phase, RCA, 1950s.

crucial figure in Fletcher's development as a successful graphic designer. Paul Rennie has written of Fletcher that it was while he was studying at Central that he learned from the posters he saw on the Underground, considering those by Eckersley as 'magical'. Rennie wrote:

> Fletcher instantly abandoned his John Minton period, which had been preceded for a while by his Bawden period, and began his Eckersley period. Years later he wrote that he was probably 'still in it'.

But even after Hammersmith and Central it would appear that Fletcher was not entirely sure what the next step should be, for he suddenly departed

for Barcelona, finding temporary employment as a teacher of English at a Berlitz language school. When he returned, he clearly had decided to stay with 'art' and furthered his formal education by study at the Royal College of Art, by now a mature twenty two year old.

What the Royal College brought to Fletcher (besides what additional knowledge and skills he derived from the course itself) was a scholarship to Yale School of Art and Architecture, and it was this American adventure that was to set the seal for him, to give him his first firm foot upon the ladder. He was fortunate enough to arrive at Yale for his two year post-graduate training not long after Josef Albers took over the reins as Head of the Department of Design, with the likes of

RAFAEL KUBELIK

conducting

The Vienna Philharmonic Orchestra

Brahms: Symphony No. 4 in E Minor Opus 98

DECCA RECORDS

BRAHMS

Decca long playing 33⅓ r.p.m. microgroove full frequency range recording

Top: Alan Fletcher using typography as a central design feature, Decca Records, 1957.

Above: Witty bus graphics created for Pirelli, designed by Fletcher/Forbes/Gill, 1962.

Right: Pirelli advertisement, designed by Fletcher/Forbes/Gill, 1963.

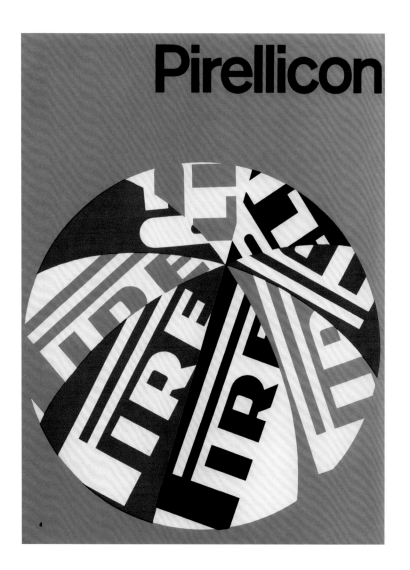

Pirellicon

Alin Eiseman and Paul Rand in his team. Albers, although with Bauhaus experience, took an altogether more relaxed approach to design and design education: 'what counts is not so-called knowledge of so-called facts but vision-seeing'.

Echoes of this view are found in Fletcher's own assertions: 'Every job has to have an idea. Otherwise it would be like a novelist trying to write about something without really saying anything.' But for Fletcher the idea was not sufficient in itself, it needed to be pushed to the edge, and this is what America gave him – the freedom and ethos to become less inhibited. Uninhibited is not a word that is often found when it comes to designers, but for Fletcher it allowed him to give an extra twist, a magical addition, to the core idea. America gave him the confidence to do his own thing, not infrequently in spite of clients' expressed needs – it helped him develop a transatlantic wit and design sophistication.

Fletcher saw Paul Rand as a particularly strong influence, someone who introduced him to graphic design for corporate imaging which Rand was pioneering in America from the 1950s; and additionally someone who helped Fletcher gain commissions, even while he was still a student: 'When I was at Yale, Rand helped me by giving me the odd freelance from IBM and introduced me to other people.'

Fletcher virtually began his career in New York, working also for projects in Chicago, Barcelona and Milan. By the time he returned to London in 1959 he described himself as with: 'a portfolio full of colour jobs and ambitious hopes'.

In London he met up with his old student friend Colin Forbes, and they started working on commissions together. It was when Bob Gill arrived from America to join an advertising agency and contacted Fletcher, who, while at Yale, had tried to meet up with him as an interesting graphic designer, that Pentagram was born. Pentagram was to become the leading design consultancy in the world. Forbes was to lay down its' modus operandi, Gill provided practical support, and Fletcher, a sort of maverick, had the playsome wit and ideas that were to attract the largest commissions. America gave Fletcher an original, highly personal, uninhibited style and for him, as with so many other designers, his work became not just a series of jobs, but a way of life.

becoming a three-dimensional designer

The term 'three-dimensional design' seems to have been coined when a new qualification – the National Diploma in Art & Design was introduced in 1961. For this, 'Fine Art', 'Graphic Design' and 'Textile & Fashion' fell into simple, relatively discrete categories, but what to do with all the other subjects offered by art colleges? Jewelry and metal work were sometimes linked together, display and exhibition design, furniture and interior design, and so on; for the new diploma, for convenience, they were all lumped together. And in this section, they are similarly grouped, a rag-tag of 'three-dimensional' would-be designers, as dissimilar as those designing for the theatre and those designing for mass production.

Furniture making had long featured on the syllabus of art and specialist colleges as a craft, as at the London College of Furniture (emerging from Shoreditch Technical College) and the colleges in furniture manufacturing districts, as High Wycombe. Pevsner, in his survey of industrial design in 1937, wrote approving of the

Opposite: Illustrated map of the Festival Pleasure Gardens, Battersea, by E.W. Fenton, 1951.

A wardrobe and circular table designed by students from the Shoreditch Technical Institute, 1935.

Shoreditch courses, which were to have such alumni as Frederick Parker (of Parker Knoll) and Lucian Ercolani (of Ercol), both of whom were to become standard bearers in the mass market. The College was offering training in interior design long before Hugh Casson set up his office at The Royal College of Art; it was closely linked to the furniture trade, while the Royal College was still wallowing in craft and ornamentation. Robin Day, at the Royal College, found what was on offer totally inadequate and inappropriate for the industry. Dick Russell, when he became Professor of Wood, Metals and Plastics at the College, complained that the length of the courses on offer was totally inadequate to develop students into full-blown designers. Gordon Russell, his brother, who was not formally trained, described his self-education as a furniture designer: 'by hand and sweat we found our own solutions as we went along'. Training provision was very patchy. Trial and error was also the way for young furniture designers not only for early learning but when seeking work; Ernest Race described his 'win some, lose some' efforts:

> ...a free-lance furniture designer in Britain tended, with a few exceptions, to have to peddle sketches of sideboards and wardrobes round High Wycombe and the East End of London.

For young furniture designers seeking role models, visits to the galleries of the Victoria & Albert Museum would give way to visits to

Above: Furniture designs created by students from Leeds College of Art (main image), and Bolton Municipal School of Art (right), 1935.

the handful of 'modernist' furniture shops as the long established Heal's of Tottenham Court Road, Bowman's in Camden Town, Woollands of Knightsbridge and, later on, Dunn's of Bromley.

When it came to the training of 'industrial' designers the Americans were well ahead with such professional pioneers as Raymond Loewy, Walter Teague and Henry Dreyfuss. Loewy, by 1936, had set up a London office managed by Douglas Scott who had actually studied silversmithing at Central in the 1920s. It was, in fact, at Central that one of the earliest courses in industrial design in Britain was developed in 1938, named 'Design for Light Industry', only renamed 'Industrial Design' in 1946. A.E. Halliwell and William Johnstone had begun to hatch the idea of such a course at Camberwell School of Art when the war intervened, but were able to develop their ideas further when both came to Central. Johnstone

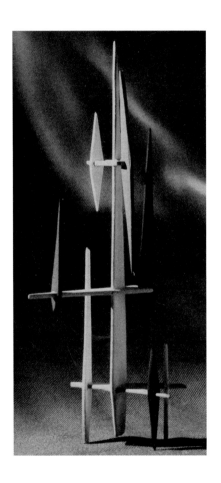

would claim: 'the seeds for the future training of the modern industrial designer in this countrywere sown at Camberwell'.

The Royal College, described as a 'somnolent backwater' when it came to industry, was not to offer a full-blown course in industrial design until Misha Black was appointed as Professor in 1959, steering the development of industrial design education whilst in post there until 1975. It was perhaps worth the wait as Black was to become an evangelist for the subject, seeing it as 'celebrating the dignity of man'! It was not until 1959 that Desmond Skirrow, writing in *Motif 3*, felt able to draw a picture of:

> ... young men pronouncing themselves capable of designing anything from a playpen to a guided missile are flooding out of art school like bubbles from a clay pipe...

In training for industrial design educational establishments had lagged behind, for, by the end of the WWII, the Council of Industrial Design had been established and, indeed, already felt able to mount its 'Design at Work' exhibition in 1948, subtitled 'an introduction to the industrial designer, with a study of his methods of working and the position he holds in industry today'.

A number of reasons account for industrial design coming late when it came to designer training, and consequently late as a design profession. One was that no one was too sure where such training should be lodged, whether in an art school or in a technical college

Opposite: An exercise in abstract form created by an Industrial Design student at Central School, 1957.

Above: Albert Halliwell, the thinker behind industrial design courses at the Central School of Arts and Crafts, 1948.

Above right: Students from the Industrial Design course at work, 1963.

– in the former bringing technology to the artistic student, or in the latter bringing aesthetics to the engineering student. Leicester College of Art was a rare early example of sharing its site with a technical college, the two sets of students being able to mix with a common library, canteen and gym. Even with the coming of Polytechnics where art and technology were administratively combined, the two were rarely on the same site.

And then there was the problem of the machinery and equipment considered necessary to make training for industry realistic, being beyond most colleges' budgets and physical space. Robin Darwin in his report on the training of industrial designers, completed before his appointment to the Royal College, actually suggested an entirely new kind of educational establishment resembling a small factory, one that would offer furniture and interior design and display work along with plastics and light engineering (the melee to be grouped as 'three-dimensional design'), but this was never taken up.

lucian ercolani

1888–1976

Ercolani has been included not so much for originality or radicalism of his designing, but because what he designed was so popular, produced for a mass market, to be found in so many homes in the 1950s and '60s; and because his career followed a fairly conventional path, unlike that of many of the other young designers included.

Ercolani had been born near Urbino in Italy, but the family moved to London when he was about ten, settling in Walthamstow. His father, trained as a cabinet maker, then running a picture framing business, made the move hoping to better his career. He took a job as a carpenter for the Salvation Army, which was, in its turn, to play a key part in his son's career. Ercolani attended the Salvation Army School and, on leaving when fourteen, also started to

work for the organisation, initially as a messenger boy. His progress at school had been poor, largely because of his limited knowledge of English, and he had been bullied, perhaps because of this; he has been described as desperate to leave. Once in work, and encouraged by his parents, he started to thrive, attending evening classes in furniture making at the Shoreditch Technical Institute. By 1906 he had been promoted to the Salvation Army joinery department in which he stayed for some six years (also playing the trombone in the organisation's band).

Along with his relatively routine work and his studies for the City & Guild's certificate on the theory and construction of furniture, Ercolani spent what spare time he had reading up on furniture and art at the Shoreditch library and making

A music cabinet designed and made by Lucian Ercolani at Shoreditch Technical Institute, 1907.

visits to the Victoria & Albert Museum. Although some of the projects he was involved in at the College tended to the ornate, as a pearl inlaid music cabinet, Ercolani's tastes were beginning to veer towards simplicity.

Aged twenty one he felt he needed more challenge and found himself a job at Frederick Parker & Sons in High Wycombe, then the centre of chair making. He recorded that one of his early assignments was to design a four-poster bed a la Chinoise Chippendale! But he found the company's considerable library and its outstanding furniture collection a good source for extending his background knowledge to his trade. He became noticed for his enthusiasm and work ethic, and, in 1912, only in his early twenties, he was asked to give evening classes on furniture design at High Wycombe Technical Institute.

One of his evening class students was Edward Gomme. Ercolani began to give him private tuition and to become friendly with his family who offered him lodgings as he had been travelling daily from Walthamstow. The Gomme's had a furniture manufacturing business (later to produce G-plan), and soon Ercolani had switched jobs to become

Chairs for my customers
—*hip-pip hooray!*

" My latest dining version of the traditional Windsor Chair," *said the ERCOLion,* " is causing many people to sit up in comfort and take notice. It retains all the endearing and enduring virtues of its kind, but garnishes them with new graces and refinements. Note the pleasing proportions, the mellow waxed finish and the detachable pallet cushions which successfully avoid shining after-effects no matter how often you sit on them. My chairs are designed with the tenderest consideration for the sitter's anatomy (and his pocket) in either natural or dark wood. All good furniture shops get a supply. Call it a policy of chair and chair alike, or better still call at your nearest stockist and see them for yourself."

FURNITURE INDUSTRIES LIMITED · HIGH WYCOMBE · BUCKS

Ercol advertisement, *House & Garden,* 1953.

a designer for the Gomme's. He recorded of the change: 'Design was first and foremost in my mind but they wanted to call me manager.' And design he did, but not quite the design he had been trained for as, with the onset of war, he found himself designing for the Ministry of Munitions and for de Haviland. Nevertheless all this experience was to extend Ercolani's technical know-how for the use of machinery to mass produce wooden products.

At the end of the war his relationship with the Gomme's soured when, with a reorganisation of the firm, his progress was blocked and he did not get the directorship he expected. His frustration, and indeed anger, at this triggered him to start out on his own. In 1920, along with investors, Furniture Industries Ltd. was established.

Lesley Jackson, his biographer wrote: 'It was apparently his determination to overcome insurmountable odds that unlocked his creative potential and commercial drive.' His determination was fuelled by an outstanding dynamism – sheer energy. Paul Ferris wrote of Ercolani's style:

He is always seen running, jumping, gesturing, banging his hat on the table, talking non-stop, throwing things, exploding with wrath one minute and apologising the next.

This may well say more for his cultural background than his design motivation, but it drove the company forward. In 1928 it adopted the name Ercol. Unmotivated by personal gain, operating frugally, and doing much of the early designing himself, Ercolani built up a company employing several hundred people, producing increasingly simple, unadorned Shaker-like furniture, similar to that he had admired on a trip he had made to America. His standards and reputation were such that his was one of the first companies to be approved for the WWII Utility Furniture Scheme, when the Board of Trade ordered some hundred thousands chairs from him. When better times came in the 1950s and '60s Ercol was producing two thousand pieces of furniture a day.

Ercolani's achievement was to develop the technology for mass production – but mass production of good design. His family may have set him in the direction, providing stability for his early learning, but it was to be Parker's and Gomme that were to challenge his design potential.

gordon russell

1892–1980

At the turn of the nineteenth into the twentieth century a young lad might have been found looking out from his school's dormitory window, sketching the charming architecture he could see around him in Chipping Camden, one of the architecturally attractive small towns in the Cotswolds, whose buildings, albeit much admire by the young sketcher, would probably have gone largely unnoticed by his fellow pupils.

> I never cease to be grateful to my unknown but deeply revered teachers; the builders of these little Cotswold towns and villages. I came to them to learn and they taught me many things for lack of which the world would be poorer today…how to handle fine materials with respect…to employ direct workmanlike methods and to try to apply the test of honesty to all work and action.

Russell's father was key to his career development as much by his own enthusiasms as by direct guidance. On reflection Russell wrote:

> I suppose it must have been my fascination in observation and analysis which led me on the path of design…for I had no formal training but was indeed fortunate in my background, which I think tremendously important.

Russell's father was an agent for the Samuel

An early Gordon Russell design for a single oak bed, c. 1911.

Allsopp & Sons brewery in Burton-on-Trent. His work involved visiting public houses linked to the brewery and on one such visit he came upon the Lygon Arms in Broadway. He immediately envisaged it being developed into 'ye olde' hotel, and, failing to convince his employers of the idea, bought it himself. He planned to restore it and fill it with appropriate antiques to make it a classy tourist hostelry, and it was this that was to start Russell on his career as a furniture designer and eventually an arbiter of national design standards.

Russell was a weekly boarder at Chipping Camden Grammar School which was too far away for him to be a day boy. He did not find his schooling particularly stimulating, albeit he made his first piece of furniture there in the woodwork class. Yet his description of his weekly walk home on a Saturday tells much about the openness and liveliness of his mind at the time, which he described as that of a 'voracious gazer': '…there were so many things to investigate on the way, such as men at work on various interesting jobs, birds nests, cider making'.

And it was the craftsmen working near his father's hotel that were to provide the major learning

Experimental dining room furniture designed by Russell, 1929.

resource for the young Russell. Father Russell, because of his need to restore old furniture that he bought for the hotel, set up a workshop that was to morph into both a workshop and an antique furniture business. On leaving school, aged fifteen, Russell found himself working alongside a skilled foreman, Jim Turner, in his father's workshop. Although he confessed to being quite clumsy with his hands his mind was whirling: 'Day after day as I watched the work in hand, I became more knowledgeable and critical.'

Father Russell's interests were extensive including, as well as furniture and furnishings, photography and printing. Such interests were shared by his son, who 'built' himself a little 'writing' room, where, interested in calligraphy, he penned out poems that attracted him; pursuing this interest he was to help his father compile a little publicity book for the Lygon Arms. Russell also, at that time, joined a small local life drawing class:

This meeting of makers in so many different crafts was very important to me for it fired my imagination to try my hand at designing various things…I was always

going off at a tangent and designing the most improbable things, with the complete assurance of youth…I have always learned by looking, handling and experimenting rather than by any formal instruction…I read every book on architecture, furniture and decoration I could get hold of…I never remember being bored.

WWI saw Russell enlisted in the Worcestershire Regiment, and serving on the front line where he was wounded. It brought him horror at the senselessness of war but it also gave him the experience of commanding, delegating and inspiring – ingredients for his later career roles. In an official service book he signed himself as 'designer of furniture' suggesting that he had given his career some thought during his service.

On his return to the Lygon Arms his father decided to make him, and his brother Don, partners in the family enterprise. Russell started to test his designing skills and also, alongside, to see to the skills development of his workshop employees. Others were to help him in this – John Gloag, the then assistant-editor of *The Cabinet Maker*

GORDON RUSSELL

opens a new kind of furniture shop at 28 Wigmore Street

FURNITURE in Oak, Walnut, Mahogany, Cherry Wood and Yew Tree may be seen at the shop that was opened to-day at 28 Wigmore Street. Designed by Gordon Russell, this furniture is made at Broadway, Worcestershire, by men who understand how wood should be used and chosen. It respects tradition without apeing antique styles.

Whether you spend £15 or 15/-, or just visit the showrooms without buying anything, you will find there ideas worth something to your home. Modern pottery, glass, metal-work and fabrics can also be seen at 28 Wigmore Street, W.1. Telephone : Welbeck 5241. (And at Broadway, Worcestershire.)

GORDON RUSSELL LIMITED

published photos of Russell's early furniture designing; Percy Wells, a distant relative and Head of Cabinet Making at the Shoreditch Technical Institute, helped with the training of some of the workmen; and a local gallery owner put on show some of his pieces which were, by chance, seen by a representative of the Board of Trade. He invited Russell to show in the Palace of Arts at the British Empire Exhibition of 1923 and in the British Pavilion of the Paris Exhibition of 1925. By the mid-1920s the Russells were employing some thirty workmen; and by 1929 Gordon Russell Ltd had a retail outlet in Wigmore Street in London.

Russell was eventually 'dislodged from his designing stool' by managerial responsibilities, firstly with his own business; then in WWII, setting standards for the nation heading the Furniture and Furnishing Production Committee as part of the Board of Trade's Utility Committee; and, finally, in the post-war years, serving as Director of the Council of Industrial Design, steering the nation's taste. The unqualified, self-taught youth came to receive honours from universities, from foreign royalties, and a knighthood from his own. In 1982 Nikolaus Pevsner wrote of Russell's career:

...making the best furniture by hand, selling the best modern fabrics and other furnishings with it, making the best modern furniture by machine, selling through others, designing furniture on a national scale, and so in the end directing a whole movement towards good modern design – no personal development could be more logical and more satisfying.

oliver messel

1904–1978

Oliver Messel, as he was growing up, did not have the slightest thought of becoming a designer, let alone a major designer for the stage and the screen. Born in Sussex in 1904 to a family that was comfortably off, it was planned that he follow his father to Eton. His father was a distinguished career soldier, yet one with an interest in the arts, who would take his son to museums, a favourite being the Victoria & Albert. And there was art in Messel's background for his mother was the daughter of the cartoonist and illustrator Linley Samborne, well-known for his long career with the satiric magazine *Punch*, as well as for general magazine, advertising and bookwork.

As preparation for Eton Messel boarded at Hawtreys, but he recorded little on his time there, or indeed at Eton, merely to write: 'I did nothing at school. I was no good at anything at school.'

This seems to preclude the more usual confession of would-be designers that they at least found solace in the art room or workshop. Yet it was noted of Messel as a youth that he could make anything from anything, including crocheting hats for his mother! In spite of his protestations, Messel must have shown a more than average competence at art while at Eton, for his father sought advice on his son's career from a friend, Walter Archibald Propert, who owned the Claridge Gallery, and was a well-known balletomaine. Propert not only exhibited theatrical designs but had, at about that time, written a key work *The Russian Ballet in Western Europe 1909–1920*. In Propert's

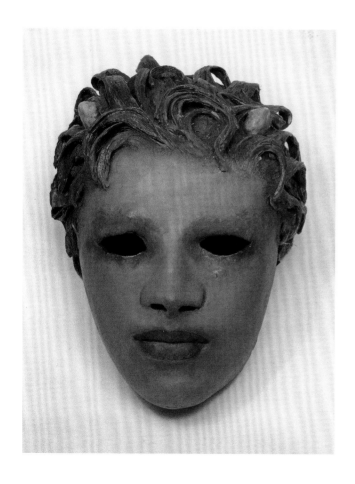

estimation young Messel's talent warranted a time at art school, and so, in 1922, Messel was enrolled at the Slade School of Fine Art, part of University College, London.

Yet, as with Eton, Messel felt out of tune with what was on offer, which seemed to him to be mainly boring life drawing classes when he was developing an interest in portraiture. Yet it was possibly this boredom that led Messel and a fellow student, Rex Whistler, to start, on their own, to experiment with mask making. Unbeknownst to him, this was to be the 'open sesame' to a career in which he was so to distinguish himself. These masks where not just cut out pieces of cardboard, but were sophisticated in their structure, modeled from waxed casts with layers of flour-pasted paper (much as papier-mache) and highly decorated. Of his time at the Slade, Messel wrote:

> I never thought of having anything to do with the theatre. I merely trained as a painter at the Slade. The curious thing was that in my time there there were no such things as schools of theatre design, or anything like that. We just went to study

to paint, and if anyone was given a job to do for the theatre they did it or didn't...

In this Messel was roughly correct, for Wimbledon School of Art, which was to be considered a specialist school for the theatre and the performing arts, only started a theatre design course in 1932. And although theatre design was included in Central's School of Textile and Design from 1919, its separate School of Costume was not set up until 1930, scenic design only being introduced in the late 1930s.

Leaving the Slade, in 1924, Messel took up what has been described as an apprenticeship with the artist John Wells. It was at this point that Propert, who had guided Messel to the Slade, yet again made a key intervention in his life. Propert had been struck by the clever artistry of Messel's masks and included them in an exhibition in his gallery. Messel recorded:

I had some masks made on exhibition at the Claridge Gallery, in London. It was an exhibition of young artists, and they also had all the designs for an early Diaghilev

ballet. The impresario [Cochran] saw my masks and asked me to do some work for him... then everything seemed to happen at once, Cochran, who had been an actor, soon after WWI became an impresario putting on revues, musicals and plays throughout the inter-war years; he also produced Ballet Russes.

Messel, who appears to have had more than an element of snobbism to him, was at first reluctant to take commissions from the showman Cochran, but was eventually won over, and, because of the way Cochran encouraged his talent, Messel actually came to view him as a second father.

By 1925 Messel found himself designing for Diaghilev's 'Zephyre et Flore', and, from 1926, for some half-dozen years for Cochran. He was barely into his twenties, but he would not only have won commissions by his obvious talent, but by his good looks, charm and sexuality, as well.

So started Messel's career as a designer, not only for the stage, but, from the early 1930s, for film as well; his career was to span some fifty years, only interrupted by a short spell in

Right: Oliver Messel's design for a Cochran revue, 1929.

Left: Oliver Messel's set design for the film 'Romeo and Juliet', from 1936.

Camouflage in WWII. A major theatre critic wrote of him, in 1930:

> It is a pity Oliver Messel is an English-man; if he had been a Roosian or a Proosian …we should have long hailed him as a great scenic artist. As he is merely a Londoner the play-going world is content to be ravished once a year at the London Pavilion and to forget all about this fine artist until Mr. Cochran's next reminds us.

In designing for performance Messel had to learn to compromise, not only with the intentions of the author or script writer, but with the opinions of the director, along with the challenge of space and budget. His approach was not that of an 'intellectual' designer (a theorist, like Gordon Craig) and some critics saw his designs as not much more than pastiche. Yet for half a century he was to tower over the British theatrical scene, his only near competitor being Cecil Beaton. In spite of his 'old family' background, his public school education and his alignment with 'Society', Messel proved to be a hard working, hands on, designer. Although working with assistants, Messel, himself, spent hours on researching references and sketching, with endless trials with models which he constructed himself, down to the last detail. He was reluctant to explain why he did what he did, with no attempt at intellectual explanations; he just let his designs speak for themselves.

During his long career Messel designed for most of London's large theatres, for over fifty productions; for operas at Glynebourne; and for some ten films. And his versatility showed itself in designing for textiles (particularly for Seker who was on the board at Glynebourne); for interior design as for the Dorchester Hotel; and, after he went to live in Barbados for his health, he converted himself into a more than amateur architect.

His achievements were recognised by University College, which awarded him a Fellowship in 1956, and in him receiving a CBE in 1958. For someone who started out merely making masks for fun, helped along the way by Mr Propert, Messel became the most distinguished British designer in his field in the mid-twentieth century.

james gardner

1907–1995

James Gardner, one of the leading British exhibition designers of the post-war years, was born and brought up in London. He seems to have lacked academic interests of any kind at school, but filled his early years sketching and scribbling a variety of war transporters, as u-boats and bi-planes; or cartooning his teachers to the delight of his fellow pupils. Colour held no charm for him, he was a black and white doodler. His parents, noticing his relative strength in artistic activities, got him some private tuition with a local artist, and eventually Gardner gained a scholarship to art school.

In the late 1920s, there were a number of well-known and stimulating artists teaching at The Westminster School of Art. Enrolled, Gardner described his aim as 'programming my eye and hand to become precision instruments'. The course he followed seems to have been along traditional lines – basic exercises with cylinders and cubes and such like, then on to drawing antique plaster casts, to progress to life drawing with some history of art along the way.

It was while he was at Westminster that Gardner began to think vaguely about a career in what was then called 'commercial art'. He was later to record his attitude to such a choice: 'In Art, painting a pudding has equal status with a nude backside, it's the same conjuring trick.' Commercial Art, for Gardner, was not just a second best to being a 'fine' artist; it was a positive choice.

In one respect, it was a lucky break for Gardner when a visiting inspector to the art school

HOW THEY FLY

James Gardner
describes with pictures and diagrams
how flying creatures, man's early devices
and the giant air liners have evolved

A COUNTRY LIFE BOOK

James Gardner's book cover design for Noel Carrington of Country Life, 1939.

told him of a job going at Cartier, the jewellers. Unlike other students, he did not have a period drifting around, looking for work, for on leaving Westminster, he immediately found himself sitting at a table, with the eagle-eye of Jacques Cartier upon him. In another respect it was not a particularly useful period for testing his talents, given colour did not mean much to him, and jewelry even less. Nevertheless he appears to have progressed sufficiently to be moved to the firm's design department where he claims, in his facetious style of writing, to have designed a tiara for Dame Nellie Melba. Finding the work constraining, he continued taking classes at Westminster in the evening with Bernard Meninsky and Randolph Schwabe.

After some six years the constraint became too much and Gardner 'dropped out' and had a period: 'wandering and wondering'. On his return and with little positive response to him circulating his portfolio, he joined The Carlton Studio in Great Queen Street. Established in 1926, it had grown into the leading commercial studio in Europe, carrying some forty artists. Gardner signed a three year exclusive contract, albeit that did not appear to deter him from getting some free-lance work with

an outside agent to gain extra commissions.

'I became the studio "stand-in" for any senior artist who was too busy or indifferent to take a job on.' However irksome this may have been for Gardner at times, working with the Carlton Studio gave him very varied experience both as to the type of commission and the media. One such commission was for Short's Brothers, who were launching a flying boat. Working on this stimulated Gardner's interest in all things aeronautical, leading him to research the subject and to go on to become a glider pilot. This experience was to stand him in good stead; in fact it was to start him in his career in exhibition design.

By sheer coincidence Shell's Publicity Manager Jack Beddington had been let down by a designer for an exhibition he was planning on Shell in the air. Gardner wrote: 'To get any place an artist needs a streak of luck and Beddington was mine.'

Gardner, with his knowledge of, and enthusiasm for flying, developed on the Short's commission, with a book he was doing for Noel Carrington *How They Fly*, and his own personal research, was ripe for Beddington's request to the studio for a substitute designer. He confidently

Below: Aerial view of Festival of Britain Pleasure Gardens, Battersea.

crowed: 'who needs a university degree when practically anything that is known (so far) is stashed away in museum libraries'.

Gardner had a real enthusiasm for tackling the Shell exhibition commission, and, given a free hand, as was Beddington's style, he used all his know-how and imagination and energy in the challenge:

> It didn't occur to me that I could delegate, so I set up shop in Carlton's basement with a jobbing carpenter, three apprentices, an aerograph machine and a glue pot, knowing that I could call on the Photographic Department for blow-ups.

Beddington was impressed with the result.

Gardner's budding career was put on hold with his service in camouflage during WWII. Yet even this gave him useful experience of activities that later he could relate to exhibition design. Back in civilian life, his success with Shell led Beddington to help him get the plum job of having responsibility for the overall design of the Design Council's exhibition 'Britain Can Make It' (BCMI),

Below: Gardner's futuristic Hovercraft design proposal for the Board of Trade, c. 1964.

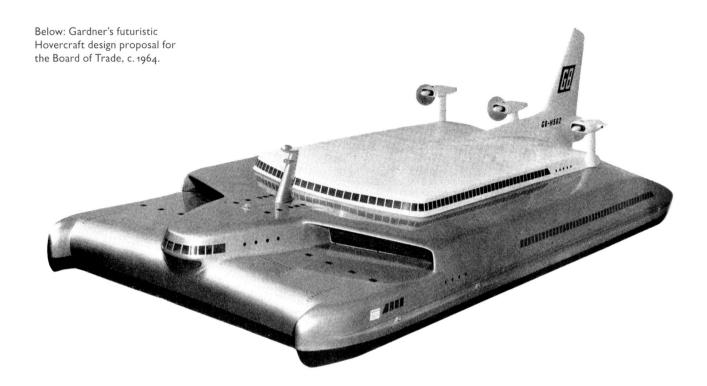

mounted at the Victoria & Albert Museum. For this, his imaginative 'scenery' helped to disguise the paucity of what Britain actually had on offer in 1946.

Gardner's foot was on the ladder! Yet not quite firmly, for when a nationwide 'cheer up' festival was proposed in the late 1940s, his name was not included, when Gerald Barry, organiser

of the Festival was drawing up his list of possible designers to commission. It was Gordon Russell, from the Design Council, who had been impressed by Gardner's work for 'Britain Can Make It', who insisted that Gardner be included in the list of designers for the Festival. It was Gardner's 'experience of a lifetime', designing the Festival's Pleasure Gardens at Battersea Park, that was to solidify his reputation as an exhibition designer, not only in Britain but across the world.

Thereafter there were relatively few international exhibitions, where Britain was to be represented, that did not bear his name as designer in some capacity or other. His showmanship in exhibtion designing spread from fairs and exhibitions, to museums, heritage centres, and the like, within Britain and worldwide. And his enthusiasm for designing around transport in the air was transferred to transport at sea with his designs for the QE2.

Gardner's work for 'Britain Can Make It' brought him an OBE. His subsequent prolific imaginative designing earned him the Chartered Society of Designers medal in 1989 for 'outstanding achievement in Industrial Design'. His joining Carlton, his commission with Shorts, being taken up by Beddington, and, through him, designing for BCMI, set a raw young jewellery apprentice on his path to becoming one of the leading exhibition designers of his time.

misha black

1910—1977

Of the designers included here, Misha Black could be said to have been born nearly fully fledged, for, by the age of seventeen, without relevant training or experience, he found himself shipped out to Spain to work on a stand for Rio Tinto Zinc in an international exhibition held in Seville. He was not only to develop into a major exhibition, interior and industrial designer, but was to proselytise the importance of design to the welfare of society both by his writing and his lecturing.

Born in Azerbaijan, by the time Black was two the family had settled in England. Although, eventually, he was wont to describe himself as an 'architect', Black had no such training, and apart from an evening class at the Central School of Arts and Crafts can be said to be entirely self-trained.

His secondary education at Dame Alice Owen School (a school of some reputation, having been founded in 1613) appears to have done little to reveal his true potential. He wrote facetiously of his time there:

> When I was a boy at school the only thing I was good at was Art. This consisted of designing wallpaper patterns which were bowlderised versions of William Morris reproductions varied by an occasional textile or dinner plate.

In the same self-depreciating vein Black claimed that the school initiated a prize for Art so that he at least should be acknowledged as being some

Below: Exhibition stand for Industrial
Rotherham, Industrial Development
Committee, c. 1932.

success. He wrote of his ambitions at the time:

> As I moved through a fog of imperceptions
> towards adulthood only one thing was
> clear, at some point I would emerge from
> somnambulistic youth to become an artist.

Black's handicap to succeeding in this aim was
that he was not, in fact, particularly good at drawing, art school was not to be on the horizon; and
although his family was comfortably off, on leaving
school he found himself: 'trailing bales of silk to
East End dressmakers and selling made-to-measure
table tops to hygienic breweries'.

With a home furnished with 'Stag at Bay' type
pictures and 'mandarin nodding' type ornaments,
Black set about his own education. He described
himself as a 'chrysallis' becoming a 'greedy moth'.
He read what he could on the then current thought
on art – Roger Fry, R.H. Wilenski and Herbert
Read; he visited galleries and museums; and he approached artists' agencies, being particularly lucky
to get a job with J. Arundell-Clarke. And with this
agency, as has been noted, at the tender age of seventeen, he was out in Seville working on a stand for

Left: Misha Black depicted in his London office, by Edward Hughes.

Opposite: Black's 'Darkness into Light' exhibition work for the Science Museum.

the Ibero-American exhibition of 1929. From the start Black was experimental in his approach, not hedged in by formal training, using photography and mobile features and other such contrivances. On his way back to England he stopped over in Paris for a time, bringing home with him dozens of sketches; and he registered on an evening class at Central – 'drawing the big toe of Greek casts'.

Eager, when it came to work, to take anything on offer, he responded to an advertisement in *The* *Times* for anyone interested in learning about shop window dressing; which led to his working in a kind of apprenticeship type relationship with one, Hans Kiesewetter. It was there that he met up with a fellow 'learner' – Lucy Rossetti. The pair, decided they could operate more favourably in partnership, and named the studio they set up, Studio Z. When Lucy fell ill Black worked on alone until 1933, ready to take any commission in hand, whether for exhibitions or general graphic design.

It was in 1933 that he joined the design group Bassett-Gray, started by Milner Gray and the Bassett brothers who had met in their student days at Goldsmith's College. From then on Black was wont to work as part of a team, not because of any feeling of dependency, but because he considered design commissions of any size benefitted from co-operative efforts. Much of Black's work (to be so frequently illustrated in design journals) has his name alongside that of others, albeit he could well have been the senior on the job. This preference for cooperative effort, in fact, meant that Black built up a considerable network of like-minded designers both in Britain and internationally. He well-understood that such collaboration did not come without pain:

> Design groups should not be happy families acquiescent to a father-figure leader. They should be disturbed by theoretical differences and opposing creative convictions; their members should be passionate in their criticism of their colleagues work and hot- tempered about their personal rights and dignity ... The fact that a group

stays in existence is proof of its validity,
but its calm outer face must conceal inner
conflicts.

Bassett-Gray morphed into the Industrial Design Partnership which shut down with the onset of war, but was revived in a new form by Black and Gray in 1944 – the Design Research Unit (DRU) – a design group with which Black was to be associated for the rest of his working life, although this did not prevent associations with other groups. His work with MARS (the Modern Architecture Research Group) perhaps gave him an excuse to refer to himself as an 'architect', leading others to describe him as such, and to his membership of the Institute of Registered Architects.

It was with DRU that Black added to his burgeoning reputation as an exhibition and interior designer the role of industrial designer, from radio and television cabinets and heaters to designing for the railways. His exhibition work, both internationally and nationally (particularly for 'Britain Can Make It' in 1946 and for the 'Festival of Britain' in 1951), brought him professional recognition. He was made Master of the Faculty of Royal Designers for Industry in 1974, was nominated President of the Design and Industries Association, and was President of the International Council of Societies of Industrial Design. Additionally he became the first professor of Industrial Design at the Royal College of Art, a post he held from 1959 to 1975. Avril Blake wrote of his progress: 'It had been a long way for Cinderella and he had had to be his own Prince Charming'. A curious muddling of the sexes but the meaning is clear. It could be well argued that Black started on his distinguished design career at the age of seventeen, but it was when he joined Bassett Gray that he found himself in exactly the right milieu, both socially and morally, in which he flowered so brilliantly.

Opposite: Design for British Railways with J. Beresford Evans and engineers of BR Western Region, 1964.

robin day

1915—2010

Although Day was born in High Wycombe, and would therefore have grown up surrounded by timber yards and furniture workshops, he did not have a family background in the industry, his father being a policeman.

His parents realised fairly early on that he was creative, and, at the age of thirteen registered him as a 'junior day technical student' at the High Wycombe Technical Institute. And, indeed, this seems to have been an appropriately stimulating milieu, for he was to win a drawing prize each year he was there, and a scholarship to study art at High Wycombe School of Art. Although this was termed an art school it inevitably was biased to turning out fodder to work in the drawing offices of the local furniture manufacturing companies. Nevertheless

Day seems to have been able to benefit from a fairly broad syllabus which included graphics, exhibition and interior design, albeit he too ended up in one of the local drawing offices, that of George Large & Sons. The actual design content of his work there was slim, largely modifying existing designs, but at least he would have familiarised himself with what was involved in furniture manufacturing. From his own interest and motivation he continued his design studies in evening classes.

One of his evening class tutors, concerned that he should make fuller use of his talents, encouraged Day to apply to the Royal College of Art, which he did; and entering on a scholarship in 1934, had high hopes of what such an elite establishment would offer. He found the reality disappointing as,

with William Rothenstein at the helm, the bias was towards 'fine' art rather than design.

> The RCA was a great let-down. I felt lost, isolated and confused. My tutor, Professor Tristram, was a specialist in the restoration of medieval frescoes. There was tuition in fine arts and crafts design but nothing for product design, furniture design and interior design, and there were no workshops except for textiles and pottery.

Day felt he would have to do much of his educating himself and to this end searched out relevant books and magazines, visited museums, libraries and exhibitions, and frequented the more progressive furniture shops. His work for the College diploma earned him a continuation scholarship for a fourth year.

He left the Royal College determined to become a free-lance designer and managed to survive by getting small commissions, supplementing these earnings by part-time teaching at various suburban art schools. It was at Beckenham Art School, where he had been asked to prepare a course on three-dimensional design, that he was assisted by Clive Latimer, who was later to prove key to Day's development as a furniture designer.

Exempted from National Service during the war, as being asthmatic, Day continued with his commissioned work and his teaching. His career path was slightly repositioned when he began

Above: Robin Day and Clive
Latimer's prize-winning storage
unit, 1947.

Right: Day's seating system for
Hille, 1960s.

teaching at the School of Architecture at Regent Street Polytechnic. There, a fellow lecturer, Peter Moro, involved Day in some of his commissions which were largely to do with exhibitions. Day, who was continuing his self-education by taking up typography, contributed with exhibition posters and graphics. This experience led to his gaining commissions for himself in this area, and, indeed, Day's early reputation as a designer was from his exhibition work, albeit furniture design was still in the back of his mind.

It was in 1947 that Clive Latimer, who already had some of his furniture designs included in the 'Britain Can Make It' exhibition, contacted Day to suggest they joined forces to enter a MOMA competition for the design of 'Low Cost Furniture'. With 750 entries from 32 countries, the pair won a five thousand dollar prize with a storage unit. It was this win that was to bring Day recognition and commissions as a furniture designer, as for sections of the Festival of Britain and the seating for the Festival Hall. There followed a long-term relationship with the progressive furniture manufacturer Hille, for whom Day was to be their main designer for some twenty years, producing such iconic

designs as for the Polypropylene chair of 1963 and, for the education market, Series E in 1972.

His relationship with Hille was not an exclusive one and Day was to have similar ones as with Pye for radio and television cabinets, and with John Lewis for house styling. His work was imbued with what he termed 'evangelical zest' – he did not see designing as a vehicle for indulgent self-expression:

> It was my mission to mass-produce low cost seating, because I do think clarity, and what we call 'good design' is a social force that can enhance people's environment.

Day's outstanding designing was recognised by his receiving the Minerva Medal from The Society of Chartered Designers, being elected a Royal Designer of Industry by the Royal Society of Arts, and, in 1983, being awarded an OBE. But one wonders whether his career path would have developed in the way it did but for Clive Latimer's invitation for the MOMA competition.

epilogue

'I am not theoretician, but a
practicing designer – by nature
simple, mostly sobre and perforce
industrious.'

Milner Gray, 1986

It is clear from the small sample of young lives described here that would-be designers come in a variety of shapes and sizes, with career paths from meandering to dead straight; and that the speed at which they advance is as unalike as that of the tortoise and the hare.

At school, in mathematics lessons, one was asked to find the highest common factor (HCF) of a group of random numbers; is it, in the circumstances of becoming a designer, that HCF's can be abstracted from such a diverse crew – what did they have in common as they developed?

A predominant factor seems to have been their self-motivation. Although they may have reacted positively to suggestions from adults, it is they, themselves, who largely determined how they filled their time – collecting, sketching, making and modeling, building creative dens for themselves at home – they were all busy bees. Conran had his burgeoning workshop, Russell his space for his calligraphy. One rarely comes across the word 'boredom' in their early lives, and, on the rare occasions it does appear, it would seem to be when enthusiasms are held back in some way.

This eager determination to try, to experiment, to find out, seems to have beeen accompanied by an amazing self-assuredness. Whether applying for jobs for which they appear to have had no relevant experience, determining their own educational programmes or setting up business on their own, they mostly are a self-confident brood. It was not a matter of smugness or of showing-off – they just

Journal of the Society of Industrial Artists, October 1953.

had this feeling that they knew, unconsciously, that they could do what they set out to do. Enid Marx pushing her way into an established atelier of textile hand printers, Muriel Pemberton setting up a design course for herself, Eckersley and Lombers, Foale and Tuffin all deciding to go free-lance immediately on leaving college, all display this inner confidence.

Knowing they could was not a matter of conceit, for generally our would-be designers were modest, some even described as humble, as even letting their work go unacknowledged. This seems to have stayed with them even after they had built up reputations for themselves. Their satisfaction lay in doing what they loved doing, not particularly motivated by money or status or likely rewards. The young Alastair Morton and Gordon Russell, both given considerable responsibility at an early age in their fathers' businesses, did not throw their weight around, but humbly learnt from those more experienced who they were being asked to supervise; and a similar unpretentiousness was shown by Jean Muir, persisting on calling herself a dressmaker in the fashion industry.

Few of our young would-be designers had remarkable academic achievements to support their

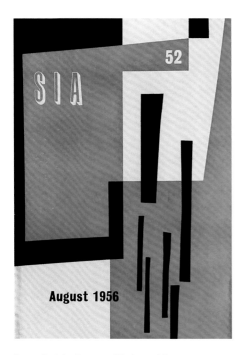

Journal of the Society of Industrial Artists,
August 1956.

ambitions. Oliver Messel was 'no good at anything' at Eton, Ashley left Christ's Hospital with no formal qualifications, most were relieved, as Marion Foale, to leave academia and try to make their way in the 'real' world. Yet although not academic, and for most not even strongly intellectual, when it came to matters that interested them there they all were, visiting libraries, museums and art galleries – getting knowledgeable about chairs or clothes, or whatever – Ruari McLean learning more from libraries than from his Edinburgh printing course, Ercolani ferreting around the Shoreditch library to extend his understanding of furniture design.

Their young minds may well not have been stimulated by what was on offer from standard educational courses, but their eyes and brains were ever alert – Conran's 'bubbling with ideas'. What Mary Quant was to describe as 'hoovering', Marion Foale called 'imbibing' – they fed on everything around them. Misha Black said of his youthful self that he was 'a greedy moth', Russell 'a voracious gazer'. Anything could be gist to the mill for them; and their need of ever to be learning, allied to their inner confidence, led many of them to seek out gurus that others would have been too in awe of

to approach – Muriel Pemberton contacting James Laver at the Victoria and Albert Museum, Ruari McLean visiting Jan Tschichold in Switzerland. Such established figures were not seen as icons by the young designers, but merely as useful aides to self-development.

Although the young designers were initially entirely wrapped up in the excitement of their specialized learning and in the testing of their imagination and skills, gradually, either consciously or unconsciously there seeped into their activities and thinking an awareness that what they were doing might have some wider significance than personal enjoyment or client satisfaction – a thread of idealism with a resulting evangelism – Jean Muir wanting to raise standards from the then current slapdash ever-changing fashion industry, Misha Black's concern for co-operative effort, Anthony Froshaug trying to persuade his fellow students at the Central School of Arts and Crafts of the beauty and importance of typography, Ashley believing that the world could be saved by good design. Standards, consumer taste, the improvement of society – these were all seeds in the minds of the newly fledged designers.

And perhaps one further attribute present in the make-up of so many of these young designers was self-discipline – the ability to curb natural exuberance, or anarchic waywardness, or ego-tripping, to meet such constraints as deadlines, budgets and client's briefs. Many mentioned that whatever else their formal design education had given them, discipline was a key element; even the rebellious Marion Foale, off down to the pub on her first day at college, reported this as an input from her years at the Royal College of Art.

Self-motivation, self-confidence in pursuing their bents, modesty, idealism, along with focus and self-discipline were all characteristics (HCF), that were present in most of our young would-be designers, along with their natural creative talents. Without such personality qualities their abilities, however outstanding, would have been unlikely to have been effectively harnessed, or might have been left to roam the wildly rocky territory of 'fine' art. Whether such qualities are similarly present in those born into the age of computers, of consumerism, of our narcissistic celebratory culture, is for others to research.

bibliography

1946   Herbert Read, 'Introduction', *The Practice of Design*, Lund Humphries.

1951   *The Anatomy of Design*, Royal College of Art.

1968   Gordon Russell, *Designer's Trade*, Allen & Unwin.

1970   Stuart Macdonald, *The History and Philosophy of Art Education*, University of London Press.

1971   Jocelyn Morton, *Three generations of a Family Textile Firm*, Routledge Kegan Paul.

1971   James Moran, *Stanley Morison*, Lund Humphries.

1980   William Johnstone, *Points in Time*, Barrie & Jenkins.

1980   James Holland, *Minerva at Fifty*, Hurtwood pub.

1980   *Jean Muir* [exhibition catalogue], Leeds Art Galleries.

1983   ed. Roger Pinkham, *Oliver Messel*, V&A.

1983   James Gardner, *Elephants in the Attic*, Orbis.

1984   Avril Blake, *Misha Black*, The Design Council.

1984   Barty Phillips, *Conran and the Habitat Story*, Weidenfeld & Nicolson.

1985   Raymond Plummer, *Nothing Need Be Ugly*, DIA.

1986   *Royal Designers on Design*, The Design Council.

1992   Jeremy Myerson, *Gordon Russell*, Design Council.

1993   James Gardner, *The ARTful designer*, James Gardner.

1993   John Russell Taylor, *Muriel Pemberton*, Chris Beetles.

1995   Nicholas Ind, *Terence Conran*, Sidgwick & Jackson.

1997   Helen Reynolds, *Couture or Trade*, Phillimore.

2000   ed. Sylvia Backemeyer, *Making Their Mark*, Herbert Press.

2000   Ruari McLean, *True to Type*, Oak Knoll Press.

2000   ed. Robin Kinross, *Anthony Froshaug*, Hyphen Press.

2001   Lesley Jackson, Robin & Lucienne Day, Mitchell Beazley.

2003   *Ashley*, National Galleries of Scotland.

2007   Sinty Stemp, *Jean Muir*, Antique Collectors' Club.

2009   Iain R. Webb, *Foale & Tiffin*, ACC Editions.

2012   Lesley Jackson, *Alastair Morton & Edinburgh Weavers*, V&A Publishing.

2012   ed. Octavia Reeve, *The Perfect Place to Grow*, RCA.

2013   Lesley Jackson, *Ercol*, Richard Denis.

2013   Ruth Artmonsky, *Enid Marx*, Antique Collectors' Club.

2018   Alan Powers, *Enid Marx*, Lund Humphries.

2020   Henrietta Gooden, *Wendy, Janey, Joanne & Madge*, Unicorn Press.

2021   Paul Rennie, *Tom Eckersley*, Batsford.

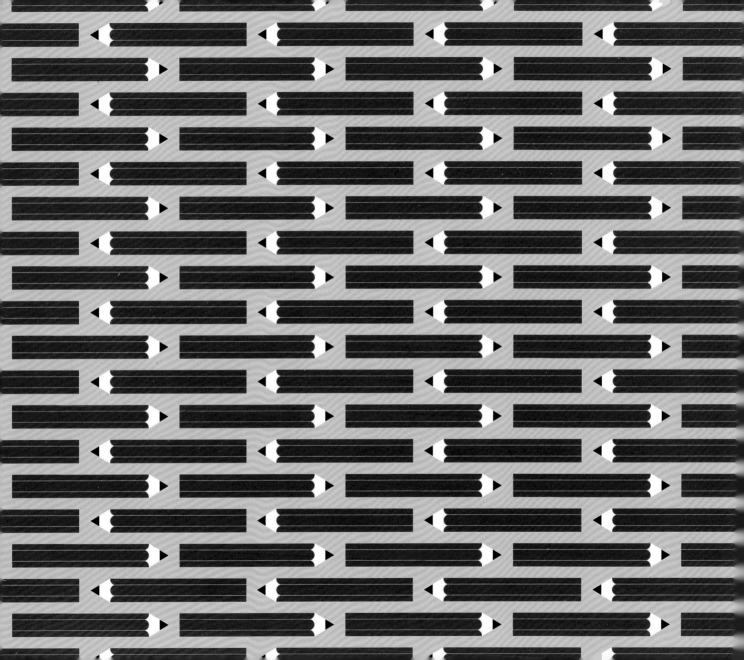